Employee Stock Purchase Plans

Employee Stock Purchase Plans

Edited by Ed Carberry and Scott Rodrick

The National Center for
Employee Ownership

This publication is designed to provide accurate and authoritative information regarding the subject matter covered. It is sold with the understanding that the publisher is not engaged in rendering legal, accounting, or other professional services. If legal advice or other expert assistance is required, the services of a competent professional should be sought.

Employee Stock Purchase Plans
Edited by Ed Carberry and Scott Rodrick
Book design by Scott Rodrick

The National Center for Employee Ownership
1736 Franklin Street, 8th Floor
Oakland, CA 94612
(510) 208-1300
(510) 272-9510 (fax)
E-mail: *nceo@nceo.org*
Web site: *http://www.nceo.org/*

Published November 2000

ISBN: 0-926902-68-7

Contents

Preface

Employee stock purchase plans (ESPPs) have become one of the main vehicles of employee stock ownership in the U.S., together with employee stock ownership plans (ESOPs), stock option plans, and Section 401(k) plans. However, there has been little information in print on how ESPPs work, what the accounting, tax, and other technical issues are, what companies are doing with their plans, and how best to communicate an ESPP to employees. This book is being published to remedy that situation and provide guidance to companies and their advisors. The introduction reviews the basics of ESPPs, while the following chapters cover the technical and practical issues that arise.

Even though a tax-qualified "Section 423" ESPP must be offered to almost all employees, it is often the case that relatively few employees participate in the plan. One goal of this book is to address why that happens and suggest ways in which participation can be increased. When there is a high level of employee ownership combined with greater employee involvement throughout the company, both the company and its employees can benefit greatly.

We hope that you find this book useful and that it inspires you to become more involved with broad-based employee ownership in its various forms. To read about the other information resources that we at the National Center for Employee Ownership (NCEO) offer, visit our Web site at *www.nceo.org* or see the back of this book.

Introduction

Ryan Weeden, Ed Carberry, and Scott Rodrick

All types of broad-based[1] equity compensation plans have become more prevalent in the last decade. Currently, through employee stock ownership plans (ESOPs), broad-based stock option plans, and Section 401(k) plans that primarily invest in company stock, over 15 million U.S. employees actively share in the stock price appreciation of their companies. Additionally, several thousand companies sponsor employee stock purchase plans (ESPPs), with over 15 million employees participating in these plans. Those numbers, however, have not translated into broad-based ownership through ESPPs; historically, most companies have seen only a small percentage of employees participate in these plans.

We are beginning to see, however, a growing interest in ESPPs, and in particular, a growing interest in how to create the conditions to encourage broad-based participation in ESPPs. ESPPs allow employees to buy stock of the company using their own money. These plans offer some unique benefits over other types of equity compensation but have their own limitations as well. Many companies are attracted to ESPPs because they allow employees to become part owners of the company by using their own cash to purchase shares. Shareholder interest groups and corporate managers are particularly attracted to ESPPs because the benefits of having employees become owners (such as getting employees more involved with their jobs and more attentive to the company's share value) are accomplished through direct purchases of stock.

The required purchase, however, can also be a barrier for many employees to become stockholders, since lower-paid employees may find it difficult to purchase shares. Consequently, ESPPs tend to have lower percentages of employees acquiring stock than other types of stock-based employee benefit plans, and companies that want to encourage broad-based employee ownership may find an ESPP a difficult mechanism to accomplish this. Furthermore, employees also tend to sell their shares as soon as they are eligible to under plan rules and tax law, possibly weakening their sense of being owners.

About This Book

Given the growing popularity of ESPPs, it is time to take a closer look at them. This book is a contribution to what we hope will be a growing body of information. It is intended to provide a concise overview of how ESPPs work; to show how to approach the process of designing, implementing, and operating them; to present the elements of a successful plan; and to report the experiences of companies with plans. Although the issues discussed in this book are applicable to ESPPs aimed at a limited number of employees, the focus is on plans that target and include a broad group of employees.

Establishing and operating any type of broad-based equity compensation requires a knowledge of the relevant legal and regulatory issues as well as an understanding of the key practical considerations in designing, operating, and communicating it. This book will help you approach these issues in a more informed way.

The first three chapters of this book, "Designing and Implementing an Employee Stock Purchase Plan," "Administering an Employee Stock Purchase Plan," and "Accounting for Stock Purchase Plans," provide a comprehensive overview of the primary regulatory and practical issues involved in establishing and operating stock purchase plans. Chapter 4, "Getting the Most Out of Your ESPP," offers insights into how companies can increase participation rates in their stock purchase plans. Finally, the last chapter, "Recent Research and Case Studies," reviews the research that has been conducted on stock purchase plans and takes a look at the experience of eight companies with stock purchase plans with high participation rates. The remainder of this introduction provides an overview of ESPPs.

What Are Employee Stock Purchase Plans?

An ESPP allows employees to purchase existing or newly issued shares of their employer, often at a discount, using their own money. Some plans simply allow employees to purchase stock using cash. Most plans, however, establish a mechanism through which employees can accumulate savings through payroll deductions over a set period of time (usually called an "offering period"). Employees use these funds to purchase stock on specified dates either at the end of this offering period or at set intervals within the offering period. Some companies match part of the employee's salary deferral with additional funds to purchase stock.

In an ESPP, employees make the decision to participate in the plan and purchase stock. The purchase price can be determined in different ways. Some plans simply use the fair market value of the stock on the purchase date. Some plans have what is known as a "look-back" feature, in which the purchase price can be determined by using the value of the stock at the beginning of the offering period or on the purchase date, whichever is lower.

For example, Company ABC has an ESPP. At the beginning of the offering period, January 1, 2000, the fair market value of the stock is $10. On the first purchase date, June 30, the stock price is at $15. If there is no look-back feature and a 15% discount, an employee can purchase the stock at $12.75 per share ($15 × 85%). If there is a look-back feature and the same discount, the employee can purchase stock at $8.50 per share ($10 × 85%). Thus, although ESPP participants use their own money to purchase stock just like any other shareholders, with a discount and a look-back feature, they often can purchase stock at a price that is substantially lower than the actual value of the stock on the purchase date.

There are two types of ESPPs: those that are tax-qualified (also known as "423 plans" or "Section 423 plans," after Section 423 of the Internal Revenue Code [the "Code"], which sets forth the requirements for them) and those that are nonqualified. Section 423 plans provide more beneficial tax treatment for employees, provided that the employee meets certain holding requirements and the company designs and operates the plan according to specific rules. Nonqualified ESPPs do not offer any special tax treatment for employees, but neither the employee nor the company has to comply with the same strict rules as a 423 plan. The company receives a tax deduction at the time of purchase equal to the difference between the purchase price and the fair market value at the time of purchase.

Nonqualified ESPPs

Nonqualified ESPPs are usually simple ways for employees to save money and purchase stock of their employer. In a nonqualified plan, any gain received by the employee at the time of purchase (from a discount and/or an appreciation in the stock price) is subject to ordinary income tax. When employees sell the stock, they pay capital gains taxes on any subsequent increase. The company receives a tax deduction equal to the amount of ordinary income recognized by the employee at the time of purchase. Although there is no prohibition from using a discount with nonqualified plans, discounts are not as common a feature as in qualified purchase plans. Nonqualified plans tend to simply offer employees the opportunity to accumulate salary deferrals and then purchase stock of the company.

Consequently, nonqualified stock purchase plans more often look like company-sponsored savings accounts that can only be used for employer securities, and the percentage of employees participating in these plans is usually lower than in 423 plans. From the employer's viewpoint, nonqualified plans can be preferable because the company receives a compensation deduction at the time of purchase equal to the difference between what the employee pays for the stock and the fair market value at the time of purchase.

Open-Market ESPPs

Open-market ESPPs, also known by such names as "broker-purchased" plans, generally are nonqualified plans in which an employee's payroll deductions are used to buy company stock on the open market without a discount. They are simple to set up and administer. A 1999 survey by the National Association for Stock Plan Professionals found that 13.6% of the companies with ESPPs used open-market plans. Given the (usual) lack of a discount and the lack of preferable tax treatment, employee participation tends to be relatively low. They are largely ignored in the literature on equity compensation, which usually emphasizes Section 423 plans when discussing ESPPs.

Qualified (Section 423) Plans

The most common type of ESPP is a tax qualified (or "423") plan. Through these plans, employees can receive more favorable tax treatment. To qualify for this tax treatment, employees must meet certain holding requirements, namely, that they hold on to the stock for one year after the date of purchase and two years after the beginning of the offering period. Also, companies must design these plans according to the requirements of Code Section 423. These requirements include:

- Only employees of the company or its parent or subsidiaries can participate.
- The right to buy stock under the ESPP must be nontransferable except by will or the laws of descent and distri-

bution, and during the employee's life, this right may be exercisable only by the employee.

- All employees must be able to participate, excepting employees with less than two years of tenure, those whose customary employment is for 20 hours or less per week or for not more than 5 months per year, and "highly compensated employees" as defined in section 414(q) of the Code.[2]

- The plan must be approved by the shareholders of the granting corporation within 12 months before or after the plan is adopted.

- The plan cannot make a grant to an employee owning 5% or more of the voting power or value of all classes of stock of the employer or its parent and subsidiaries.

- All employees must have the same rights and privileges under the plan, except that the amount of stock may bear a uniform relationship to compensation, and the plan may limit the maximum number of shares that any employee may purchase.

- Stock cannot be purchased at the lesser of 85% of the fair market value (1) at the time of grant or (2) at the time of exercise.

- Employees cannot purchase more than $25,000 worth of stock in a calendar year.

- The offering period can be up to 27 months long, unless the purchase price is determined solely on the date of exercise. In this case, the offering period can be as long as 5 years.

If all the above conditions are met, employees can take advantage of the more favorable tax treatment if they meet the one year/two year holding requirements: they do not have to pay tax at the time of purchase, and when the stock is sold, most of the gain will be taxed as a capital gain. Employees pay tax on any gain only after they sell the stock, and a significant part of this will be at capital gains rates. Part of the gain, however, will be taxed at ordinary income tax rates: the lower of either (1) the discount they received at the time of grant or (2) the total gain, i.e., the spread between the purchase price of the stock and the price at the time of sale. The rest is taxed as a capital gain. The employer will receive a tax deduction only on the amount of the gain that is taxed as ordinary income.[3]

For example, an employee begins participating in a 423 plan at the beginning of the plan's offering period, January 1, 2000. On this date, the stock price is $5 per share. The plan provides a 15% discount on the lower of either the fair market value at the beginning of the offering period or on the purchase date. On June 30, the stock price is $8, and the employee has accumulated $2,125. This enables the employee to purchase 500 shares ($2,125 divided by the discounted purchase price of $4.25). The employee holds on to these shares and sells them all on January 1, 2002, when the stock price is $15 per share, for a total sale price of $7,500. The total pretax gain for this employee would be $5,375 ($7,500 – $2,125). Since the employee met the required holding periods, most of this gain will be taxed as capital gains, except for either the lower of the discount at grant, which is $375 ($.75 discount multiplied by 500 shares) or the total gain spread at the time of sale, which is $5,375. In this case, the lower amount is $375, so the employee would pay ordinary income tax on $375 and capital gains taxes on the rest of the gain ($5,000).

If the employee does not meet the holding period requirements, a "disqualifying disposition" occurs, meaning that the transaction does not qualify for the tax-preferred treatment described above. If this happens, the employee pays ordinary income tax on the difference between the purchase price and the fair market value on the date of purchase, and the company receives a corresponding tax deduction. The remainder of the spread is taxed at capital gains rates. If we use the above example and change the sale date to January 1, 2001, then the employee did not meet the holding period. Let us say for the point of illustration that the sale price was still $15 on this new date. The total gain, therefore, would still be the same, $5,375, but the employee would pay ordinary income tax on the spread at time of purchase, which is $1,875 (500 shares multiplied by the spread at purchase, $3.75). The remainder of the gain, $3,500, would be taxed at capital gains rates.

From the employee's perspective, a 423 plan can be more attractive because of the preferential tax treatment. Many employees, however, prefer not to meet the holding requirements because holding onto the stock creates more risk. Furthermore, for lower-paid employees, the difference between the capital gains rate and their ordinary income tax rate may not be that substantial.

For employers, a 423 plan can be less desirable because the IRS requirements can be limiting and somewhat onerous to meet and because the tax deductions can be less significant than those for nonqualified plans. From an employee benefits perspective, however, many companies want to offer employees the opportunity for more the favorable tax treatment of a qualified plan. Companies that do not want to meet the various requirements of a qualified plan can design nonqualified plans that mimic the many features of a qualified plan.

Numbers of Employees Involved in ESPPs

It is difficult to estimate the number of employees actively participating in ESPPs. There is no standard requirement for companies to register these plans with the government, unlike, for example, tax-qualified plans that are covered under the Employee Retirement Income Security Act (ERISA), such as ESOPs, which must file a Form 5500 with the Department of Labor annually. Even if a company has an ESPP, this does not tell us how many employees are participating. It is ultimately the employees' right to choose whether to participate in the plan, and participation rates vary greatly. This creates a difficulty in estimating the number of employees participating in ESPPs. A company with 10,000 employees, for example, may only have 100 employees purchasing stock through its ESPP. Little research has been done regarding participation rates.

From surveys conducted by ShareData (1991), Hewitt Associates (1998), and the National Association for Stock Plan Professionals (1999) on the prevalence of ESPPs in U.S. companies, we estimate that approximately 15.7 million employees in 4,000 companies currently purchase company stock through ESPPs. To estimate the number of employees covered, we took the total number of companies offering plans, multiplied those numbers by the average number of employees in the companies (13,207 for 423 plans and 17,790 for nonqualified ESPPs), and multiplied that number by the average percentage of participation in the plans (34% for 423 plans and 17% for nonqualified ESPPs). Of the 15.7 million employees participating in these plans, approximately 11.5 million participate through tax-qualified 423 plans and the remaining 4.2 million through nonqualified plans.

In the U.S., publicly traded companies in many industries use ESPPs. Very few closely held companies have ESPPs, however, because of the administrative complexities and securities issues that arise, although we are beginning to see more companies in the pre-initial public offering (IPO) stage use these plans. Even if only a few employees participate in the plan, just the offer of a stock for purchase makes companies subject to securities registration requirements unless certain exemptions are available, and, in any case, offers always require a certain level of financial disclosure.

Private Companies and ESPPs

As noted above, ESPPs are most popular in publicly traded companies. The exception to this rule is in the case of private companies about to go public, for which it is common to introduce an ESPP concurrently with the IPO process.

Private companies face a number of issues that public companies do not in establishing any equity-based compensation plan, including ESPPs. The first issue relates to securities laws. When an employee purchases stock in a private company, the transaction is subject to appropriate securities laws relating to registration and disclosure. Most private companies will be able to meet one of a number of exemptions from the expensive process of registering their stock with the Securities and Exchange Commission. Even if the company meets one of these exemptions from registration, however, securities laws still require disclosure of more detailed financial information than many private companies are used to disclosing. (For more detail about these exemptions, see the section "Securities Laws" under "Key Issues and Designing and Implementing a Plan," below.)

Another issue for private companies is valuation. Unlike a public company, whose stock price is set by the market, a private company must decide how to value its stock. Typically, the board of directors will establish a way to value the stock, which can be accomplished through a simple process, such as using book value, or by using a more complicated valuation model. Some companies use an outside appraiser to conduct a valuation or help create an applicable method. This can be very useful in more precisely determining the value of the company and as a planning tool, but can be expensive. In companies that use book value to determine the value of its stock for the purposes of an ESPP, these plans are sometimes called "book value purchase plans." These tend to be executive-only plans. For example, managers might be able to buy stock at 75% of book value and then sell it back to the company at book value, or even 110% of book value, etc., when they leave.

Finally, unlike a public company, a private company that intends to remain private must provide a market for the stock, such as by instituting a buy-back program, if the ESPP is to be of any value to employees. This will require additional planning and some expense.

ESPPs Versus Regular Stock Options

A compensatory stock option is a contractual right to buy a specified number of shares of a company at a specified price within a specified time frame. ESPPs often are referred to as a category of stock options, more specifically being "purchase plan options" or "423 options" (in the case of 423 plans). Code Section 423 itself repeatedly defines 423 plan grants as being grants of "options." Not surprisingly, attorneys and some other practitioners tend use the same language and refer to 423 plans as simply being a different type of statutory, tax-qualified option (incentive stock options being the other type of tax-qualified option). You will see this usage in some other parts of this book.

In this introductory chapter, however, to more clearly differentiate ESPPs from "regular" options, we simply speak of purchase plans and ESPPs versus employee stock options (incentive stock options and nonqualified options). Such options are different from ESPPs in several basic ways, such as:

- An employee stock option is the right to buy stock at a stated price during a stated period; employees choose whether or not to buy stock, when to buy it (as long as the options have vested and have not expired), and how many options to exercise. In contrast, an ESPP option is the right to participate in the ESPP offering. Once the ESPP participants have signed up for the offering and indicated how much they want deducted from their salaries (in a typical plan), the company will automatically exercise the employees' options, will do so on a preset day (the end of an exercise period), and will purchase all the shares the accumulated money can buy.[4]

- Section 423 plans, which are the predominant form of ESPPs, must be offered to almost all employees, with the exceptions noted above, and cannot discriminate among those employees covered by the plan. In contrast, stock options can be offered to any arbitrary number of employees and companies can freely discriminate among employees. In general, 423 plans have more restrictive statutory requirements than incentive stock options, which are the other kind of tax-qualified "statutory options."

- ESPPs usually are paid for with payroll deductions (for which the participants typically sign up before the offering period begins), while stock options are not.

- There is no vesting associated with ESPPs (although the plan can exclude everyone with less than two years of employment, which is a somewhat different limitation), whereas stock options usually are subject to a vesting period of several years.

- ESPPs generally require more of a real investment and commitment to invest from employees than stock options. With an ESPP, employees sign up to buy stock, either at a small discount (up to 15% for 423 plans) or no discount at all. With a stock option plan, employees who are granted options need take no action unless the market price increases over the exercise price, in which case they can exercise and sell for an immediate profit.

- Another factor that makes an ESPP less of an "easy money" plan for employees is the shorter life of the plan. An ESPP offering period is commonly from 3 to 27 months, so employees will have a relatively short period for the stock price to increase. In contrast, stock options commonly have a life of 10 years before they expire, so employees can wait longer, and the spread between the exercise price and the purchase price may be proportionately higher than with ESPPs, even those with look-back provisions.

- Because ESPPs are mainly found in public companies, ESPP participants do not have the opportunity to realize the tremendous price appreciation that stock optionees in startup companies experience after a successful IPO. For plan participants, buying stock through an ESPP has less of the "easy money" windfall aspects of stock options and is a little more like investing in their own company just as one would invest in a company on the open market.

- Finally, however, there is a plus side for ESPP participants: unlike the case with stock options, which usually are not discounted from fair market value (and cannot be in the case of incentive stock options), ESPP offerings that combine a look-back feature and a discount allow employees to profit even if the company's stock price falls.

Broad-Based ESPPs

Our focus throughout this book is on stock purchase plans that at a minimum make a majority of employees eligible to participate in the plan. We recognize, however, that ESPPs are based on the voluntary purchase of shares by employees and consequently have lower participation rates than many other forms of broad-based equity compensation. Although companies can take specific steps to encourage broad participation, the choice to purchase stock is ultimately with employees.

Although there is no standard definition of what defines a "broad-based" ESPP, we consider plans that have 40%–50% participation on a rolling basis as sufficiently broad-based. Given that employees will make personal judgments, based on a number of factors, on whether they will participate in any one offering, we recognize that in any one offering period 40%–50% of employees may not be participating; therefore, if over a period of time, two to three years typically, a rotating group of employees representing 40%–50% of the workforce (a majority or close to a majority) participates in the plan, this would constitute a broad-based plan.

ESPPs can be used to promote broad-based employee ownership, but it is difficult because employees have to give up cash today to purchase stock in the future that may or may not be valuable. Companies can incorporate various plan design features that make participation more attractive to employees. A comprehensive communication program about the plan, its mechanics, and its potential benefits is crucial in promoting broad-based participation.

Plans and Plan Participation Outside the U.S.

Multinational companies frequently use ESPPs as their main global equity compensation vehicle, although it is impossible to estimate the number of employees involved. Companies with 423 plans often avoid extending them abroad; aside from any other reasons, Section 423's tax benefits are, of course, for U.S. taxpayers only, and, more importantly, the requirements imposed on stock plans by local laws in various countries can have the effect of violating Section 423. For example, Section 423(b)(5) requires that all participants "shall have the same rights and privileges" under the plan, but one country's laws may have the effect of preventing a grant on the same terms used elsewhere. Hence, a multinational corporation may prefer to use a nonqualified ESPP for non-U.S.

employees. Such companies may maintain a separate 423 plan for their U.S. employees, who can benefit from Section 423's tax advantages.

U.S. employers may also consider using locally tax-qualified plans that would simulate the plan features of a 423 plan. For instance, U.S. employers with an U.K. subsidiary might consider using a "Save as You Earn" (SAYE) plans or the recently passed "All Employee Share Ownership Plan" (AESOP) to provide preferential tax treatment to employees participating in a stock purchase arrangement. U.S. employers need to carefully assess the goals and intentions of a plan that is extended overseas.

The tax, design, administrative, and legal issues involved with extending ESPPs or other stock plans to employees outside the U.S. are beyond the scope of this book (the NCEO's book *Equity-Based Compensation for Multinational Corporations* addresses such matters). Rather, this book focuses on establishing and operating ESPPs in the U.S., although some of the broader issues discussed, such as communicating the plan, designing the plan to achieve maximum participation, and administering the plan, can apply to other countries as well.

Why Companies Use ESPPs

In the last decade, a growing number of companies have become interested in broad-based equity compensation of all types for a variety of reasons relating to labor market concerns, competitive pressures, and new organizational priorities. First, tight labor markets have forced companies to offer more attractive benefits, including equity ownership, in order to hire and retain employees at all levels. Second, the need for companies to compete in a global economy within rapidly changing marketplaces and to use the full potential of new technologies has fundamentally altered the roles employees play within business organizations. A growing number of companies realize that all employees make important contributions to the organization and that it makes sense to offer all employees, not just the highest-paid ones, a way to acquire equity. Finally, in a more fundamental sense, many companies realize that the financial well-being of their employees can translate into innumerable gains for the company and that providing employees with a way to acquire stock and share in the growth of the company is just "the right thing to do." This is particularly true at a time when returns to capital ownership have far outstripped returns to labor over a 25-year period.

Furthermore, there has been a dramatic increase in the number of companies using broad-based stock options, particularly among knowledge-based companies but also among more established nontechnology public companies. Since ESPPs are similar to option plans, their increasing popularity is linked to that of broad-based stock options. For example, we are seeing among startups that mature into more established public companies a continuing interest in providing for broad-based employee ownership. A growing number are implementing a 423 plan at the time of going public or afterwards. This is usually a way to supplement an existing stock option plan.

All of these trends have led to an increase in the number of companies interested in providing employees with some way to acquire equity, including ESPPs. There are other, more specific, reasons, however, why more companies are becoming interested in ESPPs. First, ESPPs require that employees use their own cash to purchase shares. This means that employees are taking a direct financial risk by purchasing stock. Many companies believe this is essential for making ownership really meaningful for employees. Another reason why ESPPs are attractive for companies is their favorable accounting treatment. Traditionally, companies have not been required to recognize a compensation expense for qualified ESPPs. With most ESPPs, therefore, companies are establishing a way for employees to purchase shares that does not show up on their financial statements. While these are the primary reasons why ESPPs have grown in popularity, there are other reasons, discussed below.

Minimizing Stock Dilution

One concern a company and its shareholders may have in setting up a stock plan is that the plan may dilute the equity interest of existing shareholders. The two basic factors causing dilution are (1) the issuance of new shares for the plan and (2) the discount between the purchase price and the market price.

With both stock options and ESPPs, the source of shares may be existing stock (treasury shares, reacquired shares, or shares purchased on the open market) or newly issued stock, so this cause of dilution may or may not be present. The main factor causing dilution with an ESPP is the discount from the market price. This dilution often is less than would be found under a stock option plan, however, because with an ESPP the difference in price between the date of purchase and the date of grant/enrollment is generally less, as discussed above. Thus, ESPPs do have a dilutive effect; however, it is usually far less than that encountered with stock options.

Generating Cash Flow

A second advantage of ESPPs is that they can generate cash flow by providing a way for employees to invest in the company. Publicly traded companies that issue treasury shares to meet employee stock purchases are able to leverage the existing market price of their stock as the basis for employee purchases and sell stock to employees in what may be termed miniature public offerings—offerings that avoid the investment banking fees associated with true public offerings. Employees purchase stock at a price that may be below the traded price of the stock on the date of purchase, but the company still receives the funds for corporate cash flow needs. Private companies can also take advantage of the increased cash flows associated with ESPPs by issuing previously unreleased stock or issuing new stock as needed to meet the purchase demands. These mini-"private-placements" can assist a startup company in raising incremental capital for funding necessary expansion projects on its way to an IPO or some other liquidity event.

We are starting to see pre-IPO companies or companies planning on being acquired using qualified and nonqualified ESPPs in their growth phases to simultaneously generate cash flow to the company and create another way to provide employees with equity. These companies typically use the exemption from federal securities registration requirements under SEC Rule 701, which applies to sales to employees and also to sales to certain consultants (see below).

Pre-IPO and other privately held companies typically do not have an easily ascertainable value for the shares of stock they may want to sell to employees through an ESPP; therefore, various valuation methods are used to determine how a company' stock should be priced. The buyback of the stock is usually delayed until the liquidity event is reached, which reduces the administrative complexity of the ESPP. Pre-IPO companies still have certain disclosures to make on the financial condition and risks of the company; however, most employers in these situations want employees to be aware of the value of the company in order to focus their efforts on cost-cutting and production increases.

Finally, because most employees do not have the resources to acquire shares outside of some company-sponsored plan, companies often find it necessary to institute plans that assist their employees, if not provide some incentive, subsidy, or match, to achieve widespread stock ownership. While we have seen a growing interest in ESPPs in pre-IPO companies, stock options are still the preferred vehicle of equity compensation.

Guaranteed Returns for Participants

Most ESPPs are designed to include either or both of (1) a "look-back" feature allowing employees to purchase stock at the lower price of either the beginning or end of the offering period and (2) a discount on the established purchase price. This makes ESPPs unique in their ability to return a value to employees even in a declining stock market.

Some equity compensation vehicles allow employees to receive a benefit only when stock prices increase. Stock options, for instance, become valuable to an employee only if the stock price increases above its grant price. ESPPs, on the other hand, allow employees to benefit in a declining market. This does mean, however, that the company incurs an employee benefit cost even if share prices decline.

With a discount feature, ESPPs allow employees to safely accrue savings to purchase company stock over a period of time regardless of the direction of the stock price. A comparison of two different scenarios will help explain the guaranteed benefit to employees. Table I-1 shows employees at two different companies who are enrolled in an ESPP with a look-back feature and a 15% discount on the purchase price. Company A's stock price appreciates during the offering period, while Company B's decreases.

Table I-1. Effect of Stock Price on Gain per Share

	Company A	Company B
Stock price at grant date	$10.00	$10.00
Stock price at end of offering period	$15.00	$8.00
Lower of price at time of grant or purchase	$10.00	$8.00
15% discount	$1.50	$1.20
Purchase price	$8.50	$6.80
Gain per share	$6.50	$1.20

Key Issues in Designing and Establishing a Plan

Implementation of any broad-based equity compensation strategy should be based on a thorough examination of the goals of the plan and how these goals might be met by a single compensation strategy or a combination of strategies. Do you want to set up a purchase plan in order for a broad group of employees to become stockholders? Do you simply want to give interested employees the opportunity to purchase stock? Will it primarily be an employee benefit to attract and retain employees? How important is it for employees to hold on to shares after they purchase them? Do you want to use a stock purchase plan as part of a larger strategy to create an ownership culture?

Your goals for the plan will define what your plan looks like as well as how you communicate it to employees. It is also important to look at how the plan will fit into your established structure of benefits and your corporate culture as well as who within your company will be involved in designing, implementing, and operating the plan.

For companies that really want to encourage a broad group of employees to own stock, we do not recommend that an ESPP be the sole or even primary ownership plan. Because of the discretionary basis of employee involvement in an ESPP, no company should expect to have 100% participation in its ESPP, even under ideal conditions. Most plans have a participation rate between 20% and 40%, although we have seen participation rates as high as 80%. To promote broad-based employee ownership, it is usually necessary to sponsor some type of "universal" plan that assures that a broad group of employees are able to acquire stock. It is common for companies to combine ESPPs with stock option plans, 401(k) plans with an employer match, and profit sharing arrangements.

Plan Design Considerations

The main design considerations for ESPPs include whether or not the plan will be qualified, who will be eligible to participate, how employees will purchase stock, how the purchase price will be set, the length of the offering period, the discount, whether or not the plan will include a look-back feature, and how employees will sell the shares.

Qualified vs. Nonqualified The first step is to determine whether you want to have a 423 plan or a nonqualified ESPP. A 423 plan is more favorable plan for employees but also imposes restrictions that some companies may find onerous. Furthermore, if employees take advantage of the favorable tax treatment by meeting the required holding periods, the company will not be able to take as significant tax deduction as it would be able to with a nonqualified plan. If employees do not meet the holding requirements, however, the company is able to take a tax deduction as if the purchase occurred through a nonqualified plan.

Eligibility Next, you need to decide who will be eligible to participate in the plan. If the plan is a qualified 423 plan, the law requires that most employees be eligible (see the list of

423 plan requirements given above). For a nonqualified plan, there are no rules regarding eligibility. Next, it is important to look at the level of participation that you desire. For companies that simply want to give employees the opportunity to purchase stock and do not really care about having a high participation rate, there are few design considerations. If you want to encourage the largest number of employees to participate, however, there are certain things you can do in terms of plan design that encourage greater involvement.

Increasing Participation Through Plan Design: Discounts, Look-Back Features, and Offering Periods The three plan design features that can make a stock purchase plan more attractive to employees and hence increase participation rates include (1) the discount on the purchase price, (2) the presence of a look-back feature, and (3) the length of the offering period. Obviously, the greater the discount, the more gain employees will be able to realize. The discount, however, also imposes a cost for the company and dilution for shareholders. A look-back feature creates the potential for greater gains since there is more time for the difference between the purchase price and the fair market value at the time of purchase to be larger. Again, however, this imposes a cost for the company and can have a dilutive impact on its investors.

If there is a look-back feature, the length of the offering period becomes very important, since the longer the offering period, the greater the chance for a larger spread between the purchase price and the value of the stock at the time of purchase. With longer offering periods without interim purchase dates, however, employees have less frequent opportunities to purchase stock, which may make the plan seem a more distant benefit.

All of these design features will, in effect, make the plan more or less desirable for employees to purchase stock. While there can be variation in terms of plan design features, the basic structure of most 423 plans is very similar. For example, although the rules allow for up to a 15% discount (but do not require it), most companies apply the full discount. A look-back feature is also a very common, but not required, feature. While there is some variation in the length of the offering period and frequency of purchase dates, few offering periods are longer than two years. Most plans allow employees to purchase shares either quarterly or every six months.

Securities Issues

Privately held companies that want to use a stock purchase plan must address a number of considerations that publicly traded companies have already faced. For example, they must establish a value for company stock, whereas a public company's value is set by the market. More important, however, are securities law considerations relating to registering the stock offering and providing the required financial disclosure. Most privately held companies offering ESPPs will qualify for one of various exemptions from registration requirements at the federal level, the most common of which is the exemption provided by SEC Rule 701. The exemption (as revised, effective April 7, 1999) generally applies if the aggregate sales price or amount of securities sold during any consecutive 12-month period does not exceed the greatest of (1) $1 million, (2) 15% of the company's total assets, or (3) 15% of the outstanding amount of the securities being offered and sold in reliance on Rule 701. The company should also ensure that it has complied with laws relating to securities registration at the state level. In most states, securities laws mirror federal law, but in some states they do not. Furthermore, even if the company is exempted from registration at the federal and state level, it will still have to comply with anti-fraud requirements by providing employees with certain financial information about the company.

For companies outside of the U.S., or for U.S. companies with a plan that will be implemented overseas, securities rules vary considerably from country to country. The complexities of international securities law are far beyond the scope of this chapter.

Selling the Stock

In public companies, a broker is often retained to perform all transactions for employees. In privately held companies, either the ultimate sale date is delayed until some change in control or a liquidity event occurs or the company provides a market for the shares. Private companies also normally have a "right of first refusal" to purchase the stock at some established price when an employee wishes to dispose of his or her shares. These issues are covered in more detail in chapter 3, "Administering an ESPP."

Accounting

The accounting treatment of ESPPs has been subject to the same series of reviews and modifications as other equity-based plans under the Financial Accounting Standards Board (FASB) review project of Accounting Principles Board Opinion 25 ("APB 25"). APB 25 was implemented in 1972 and for over two decades was the basis for all accounting for equity-based compensation programs in the US. Under APB 25, for most ESPPs, companies did not recognize a compensation expense for stock purchased by employees. In 1994, FASB undertook a revision of APB 25 to modify its application to current stock-based programs.

This revision process produced "Statement of Financial Accounting Standards No. 123: Accounting for Stock-Based Compensation," which required companies to either expense the value of their stock-based compensation by estimating its fair value at the time of grant or disclose in a footnote what this expense would have been. Most companies have chosen only to disclose the fair value in a footnote, which means that they still rely on APB 25 for calculating the expense on their financial statements, which in most cases is zero. Estimating what this expense would have been in the footnote as required by Statement 123 requires a detailed calculation. Although FASB recently undertook an extensive review of APB 25, and some feared this review project would result in significant changes to the accounting treatment for ESPPs, the final results, which were released in March 2000, left the accounting treatment for ESPPs the same for the most part. While in most cases an ESPP will not result in the recognition of compensation expense on the face of the financials, it is important to note that certain plan design features can trigger negative accounting treatment. It is also important to understand how the footnote required by Statement 123 is calculated. These issues are described in detail in chapter 3.

Operational Issues

Administration

Once a stock purchase plan is implemented, you will have to develop a support network to administer the plan. This includes tracking for every employee the payroll deductions, the number of shares purchased, the number of shares sold, and any disqualifying dispositions. You will need to create internal systems to manage these tasks and involve a number of individuals in various departments. Many companies use a commercial software package to help them track, monitor, and conduct reporting for these various tasks. Another alternative is to outsource some or all of these tasks. Administration issues are discussed in more detail in chapter 3, "Administering an Employee Stock Purchase Plan."

Communication

All equity-based compensation practices sponsored by a corporation should be supported by appropriate education and communication efforts. For stock ownership to have any long-term impact on employee attitudes and behavior, it is essential that employees understand the plan and how it works as well as why the company is offering them this benefit. Effective communication strategies are covered in more detail below.

ESPPs As an Employee Ownership Vehicle

Many companies hope at some level that if employees are owners, they will be more motivated and make efforts to improve company performance in their daily work, and that consequently, the company will do better. In fact, a common reason why many companies implement any type of employee ownership plan is to increase employee work effort and productivity.

While some employees who purchase stock will be more motivated, the research presents a more complex picture. The research consistently shows that employee ownership alone does not lead to increased corporate performance, and that, in fact, employee ownership alone may have detrimental effects on the performance of the company. Only when broad-based ownership is combined with a genuine commitment to create an environment in which employees are encouraged, trained, and given the opportunities to think and act like owners does employee ownership have an impact on corporate performance, and this impact can be significant. Creating this environment involves a number of common elements:

- Ongoing, meaningful ownership opportunities;
- A comprehensive communication program to explain the plan and its benefits and risks;
- Sharing financial information;
- Structured opportunities for people to contribute input about their jobs; and
- Training and education about basic business concepts, how to use financial information to make decisions, and group decision-making skills, and other relevant skills.

Certainly, companies with ESPPs can develop the last four elements. The more pressing question, however, is whether ESPPs can actually promote ongoing, broad-based ownership.

ESPPs have long been viewed as ineffective for promoting ownership attitudes and behaviors. While there is good reason for this skepticism, there is little reason to believe, however, that the innate characteristics of ESPPs prohibit them from being used as an effective ownership vehicle. It is plausible to believe that ESPPs can be used in promoting and encouraging ownership attitudes and behaviors when properly structured, supported, and communicated.

The reality, however, is that many ESPPs have only a minority of employees purchasing stock, and in most cases, employees are not holding on to the stock for very long. Why is this so? There are many reasons. Often, employees view stock purchase plans as short-term incentives, purchasing shares only long enough to reap the benefit on the discount or the "look-back" appreciation. Many companies implement ESPPs simply to satisfy their employees' needs for more benefit plans. ESPPs are relatively inexpensive to administer and implement, bring cash into the company, and can be used to complement other benefit plans. Furthermore, employees may be reluctant to participate in the plan and use their extra cash reserves to purchase stock in the company where they work.

Low participation can result from a number of other factors, including:

- *Lack of knowledge:* Employees may not understand the plan and are afraid to ask.

- *Lack of faith in the company's prospects:* Employees who do not feel their company will perform well in the future are unlikely to purchase stock in that company.

- *Employee demographics:* Younger employees have an inherently shorter time horizon than older employees while also having less ability to sacrifice current spending to purchase favorable investments. Similarly, lower-paid employees have less income and fewer opportunities to spend money on long-term incentives.

- *Plan attributes:* The presence of discounts and "look-back" features has been shown to increase participation in ESPPs. The greater the discount and the longer the look-back, the higher the participation rates.

- *General economic conditions:* If share price performance is flat or declining, employees generally do not view equity ownership favorably. Anecdotal evidence suggests one of the highest correlated attributes of participation is an increasing stock market. Of course, a plan that offers stock in an increasing market may not be offering a great discount or value to employees, whereas a share price that has recently decreased may offer a buying opportunity for them.

For ESPPs, there is no minimum participation rate that makes one plan more "successful" than another in terms of broad-based ownership. For some companies, having 25% of employees participating in a plan would be an incredible accomplishment, given their demographics and industry. For other companies, reaching 25% participation could be accomplished with very little work, and for them a successful plan would have 50% to 60% participation. Regardless, most companies would probably be happy if more employees purchased stock through the plan.

In addition to having broad participation, for an employee ownership plan to be successful in fostering the development of ownership attitudes, employees must be stockholders on an ongoing basis. For ESPPs, this depends on how long people hold onto their stock after they purchase it as well as how often they purchase stock. Anecdotal evidence suggests that employees usually do not hold on to their stock for a long period of time after purchase.

We suspect that this has mostly to do with how the plans are "sold" to employees. If employees are told that these plans provide a substantial discount from the current fair market value of the stock and they are simultaneously offered the immediate opportunity to sell their newly purchased shares back to the open market, it is not surprising that most employees sell their shares. This is especially true for lower-paid employees who may want cash for more immediate needs. If employees receive training on the financial benefits of stock ownership and if the details of the plan are communicated to employees to help them understand the benefit they are receiving, then ownership levels should be expected to rise.

One of the most unfortunate consequences of employees not holding on to their stock purchased through a 423 plan is that they forfeit the tax benefits that tax-qualified plans offer. If an employee meets the holding requirements of a 423 plan, he or she avoids income tax recognition at the time of purchase and receives favorable capital gains treatment when he or she sells the shares. Although for some lower-paid employees the difference between their marginal income tax rates and the current capital gains rate is not that significant, the appreciation they might experience on their total stock holdings (compared with a stock holding that has been diminished by paying taxes in a nonqualified plan through a share sell-to-cover arrangement) over the holding period can be substantial.

Employers that sponsor qualified ESPPs can find themselves in a difficult position. On the one hand, if employees hold'on to the shares over a period of time, they may become more involved in the company and participate more actively in its operation. This increased participation of employees coupled with an ownership stake has been proven to increase corporate profitability over time. On the other hand, if employees do not hold on to their stock purchased through a qualified plan for the required period, their gain is taxed at ordinary income tax rates and the employer receives a tax deduction equal to the taxable gain. This can be a significant benefit to the company: it writes the plan so that employees receive a discount, it is paid for the shares employees buy, it takes a tax deduction, and it passes on the ultimate cost of dilution to existing shareholders in the marketplace. From our experience, however, companies would rather have high participation in the long term than a tax break in the short term.

Increasing Participation

How do you actually transform an ESPP from a thinly subscribed, short-term compensation tool into a valued employee benefit with long-term stock ownership? As noted, certain plan design features, such as a discount and look-back feature, will make it more attractive for employees to purchase stock. Plan design features alone, however, will not guarantee higher participation rates.

Arguably, the most significant factor in encouraging broad-based participation in an ESPP is a comprehensive communication strategy. Most companies often assume that employees understand what the stock purchase plan is (and what stock is, for that matter) and that only the minimum amount of communication about the plan is needed. This is one of the surest ways to insure that your stock plan will have little meaning for employees. Although it is true that some employees have a sophisticated knowledge of stock-based compensation as well as what stock is and what affects its value, most employees have little experience with these types of plans or with owning stock at all.

Employees need to understand what the plan is, how it works, and how they can benefit from it, as well as why the company is granting them this benefit and what stock ownership can mean for them in the long run. If a company sets up a plan and assumes that employees will understand it and be more motivated, it is unlikely that the plan will have any impact on employees' attitudes or on corporate performance. Furthermore, for the plan to promote ownership attitudes, the company must support education and training efforts on financial education, basic equity ownership, and business performance issues.

Employers who sponsor ESPPs should also consider what message stock purchase plans send to employees and develop the appropriate messages into their communications programs. Remember that economists, business consultants, and financial advisors caution against putting all of one's financial eggs in one basket. When employees invest in their own companies, they rely on their employers not only for current income (from their salaries) but also for their savings (i.e., the stock they have purchased). Many employees are not able to accurately weigh the pros and cons of buying company stock as compared to alternative investments. Instead they may take a signal from the company that this is the best investment available for them, something that may or may not be true.

To educate employees about stock ownership requires a comprehensive program that uses different approaches and provides straightforward information on a regular, ongoing basis. It is essential to communicate the basics about the stock purchase plan and how employees can benefit from participating in it. It is very important to start with the most fundamental questions: How am I eligible? How do the payroll deductions work? Can I decide to withdraw? Do I have to purchase shares on the purchase dates? Do I choose how much? What is the discount? How does the look-back feature work? What are the tax consequences? How do I sell my shares? Remind them that they will get voting rights only if they purchase and hold on to the stock, provided that they receive a class of stock that has voting rights.

It is also important to communicate why employees are receiving this benefit. One of the first questions that employees will have about any kind of benefit is why they are receiving it. Employees may be suspicious of the motives and may develop their own theories about them. Why are you giving people the opportunity to purchase stock? Tell them directly why and what your expectations are of them as stockholders.

The most successful communication strategies employ many different communications vehicles to disseminate this information because different people learn in different ways. It is unrealistic to expect one form of communication to be effective in reaching everyone. Most communication techniques will fall into one of three categories: (1) printed materials, such as brochures, question-and-answer flyers, and newsletters; (2) meetings, both one on one, small group, and company-wide; and (3) electronic mechanisms, such as e-mail, intranet, and interactive voice response networks. Most companies, for example, distribute printed materials like brochures and a list of "frequently asked questions" when the plan is rolled out. Meetings and face-to-face interaction can be an effective way to communicate complicated information and to keep people abreast of developments. Finally, electronic mechanisms are becoming a popular way to provide ongoing access to plan information, facilitate transactions, and disseminate financial information about the company; in many cases, the employer gives employees access to plan documents, forms, rules, fundamentals about the plan, questions and answers about the grants, account balances, and other information through an intranet.

With the right plan features, a comprehensive communication strategy, and the creation of opportunities for employees to be involved in daily work decisions, it is reasonable to expect that companies can encourage a majority of their employees to purchase stock. And only when most employees become owners can a company can pursue the full benefits of employee ownership, such as improving corporate performance in the long term, which is why many companies have stock plans in the first place.

Notes

1. We define a broad-based plan as one in which over 50% of a company's employees actually participate.

2. Under Code Section 414(q), highly compensated employees are defined as (1) 5%-or-more owners or (2) those who earned over $85,000 per year in salary during the previous year (this dollar figure is indexed for inflation; the $85,000 figure is effective January 1, 2000) and, if the company so elects, were also in the top 20% of employees when ranked on the basis of compensation. (This is a general Internal Revenue Code definition that applies to various situations, not just Section 423 plans.)

3. At the time of this writing, the issues of federal income tax withholding requirements, as well as FICA and FUTA, with regards to 423 plans had been raised in a case pending in the U.S. Court of Federal Claims. Historically, companies have not withheld income tax, FICA, and FUTA from an employee's gain from stock purchased through a 423 plan, even for disqualifying dispositions. The IRS challenged this approach in a review of Micron Technology's 423 plan, arguing that taxes should be withheld at the time of purchase. Micron has appealed the IRS ruling.

4. However, employees may withdraw from the plan before the end of the exercise period or, if the plan permits, change the level of their participation; additionally, the purchase of shares may be limited by the number of shares the company has available or by the $25,000-per-employee yearly limit for 423 plans.

CHAPTER 1

Designing and Implementing an Employee Stock Purchase Plan

Timothy J. Sparks

This chapter summarizes the principal features of employee stock purchase plans (ESPPs) that are designed to qualify under Section 423 of the Internal Revenue Code (the "Code") and highlights some of the practical considerations involved in putting an ESPP into place, such as plan design (offering periods, contribution limits, eligibility, participation by non-U.S. employees, etc.), federal income tax issues, and shareholder approval.

The purpose of an ESPP is to encourage broad-based employee ownership of employer stock. Through an ESPP that qualifies under Sections 421 and 423 of the Code, an employee subject to U.S. tax law can purchase stock at a discount from fair market value and, if certain holding period requirements are met, receive preferred tax treatment upon sale of the ESPP shares. At the same time, under current accounting rules, the employer incurs no compensation expense for financial accounting purposes with respect to grants made under an ESPP.

Operation of an ESPP

The basic operational parameters of a tax-qualified ESPP are set by Section 423, which are discussed in greater detail below. In general, under a typical ESPP, employees are given an "option" to purchase employer stock at a favorable price at the end of an "offering period." While Section 423 does not require that the shares be purchased through accumulated payroll deductions, most employers find this approach administratively simpler than having all of the plan participants pay for the stock on the same day.

Before the beginning of each offering period, eligible employees must indicate if they are going to participate in the plan. If so, the employee typically completes a subscription agreement or enrollment form indicating the percentage or dollar amount of compensation to be deducted from his or her paycheck throughout the offering period. During the offering period, the company withholds amounts from participants' compensation and credits the amounts to participant recordkeeping accounts established for this purpose.

Under most ESPPs, the purchase price is set at a discount from fair market value. While some plans provide that the discount is to be applied to the value of the stock on the purchase date (e.g., 85% of the fair market value on that date), it is more common to provide that that discount is applied to the value of the stock on the first day of the offering period or on the last day, *whichever is lower*.

Most plans permit participants to withdraw from the ESPP prior to the last day of the offering period (the "exercise date"). If a participant does not withdraw from the plan, amounts held for his or her account under the plan are applied automatically to the purchase of shares on the exercise date for the maximum number of shares at the applicable option price. ESPP purchases often take place through a transfer agent of the company or through a brokerage account established for that purpose.

The original subscription agreement setting forth the payroll deduction percentage can continue as long as the plan remains in effect, unless the participant withdraws from the plan, becomes ineligible to participate, or terminates employment. Many plans permit participants to increase or decrease their payroll deduction percentage at any time during the offering period.

Section 423's Requirements

Section 423 of the Code sets forth certain requirements applicable to ESPPs. To qualify under Section 423 of the Code, an ESPP must meet the following requirements:

- *Employees only.* Only employees of the plan sponsor (or its parent or subsidiary corporations) may participate in the ESPP. Thus, for example, consultants and non-employee directors may not participate in an ESPP.

- *Shareholder approval.* An ESPP must be approved by the shareholders of the plan's sponsor within 12 months before or after the ESPP is adopted by the board.

- *No 5% shareholders.* Any employee who owns five percent (5%) or more of the stock of the plan sponsor may not participate in the ESPP.

- *Eligibility.* All eligible employees must be allowed to participate in the ESPP, although certain categories of employees may be excluded:

  — Employees employed less than two years;

  — Employees whose customary employment is 20 hours or less per week;

  — Employees whose customary employment is for less than 5 months in a calendar year; and

  — "Highly compensated" employees (as defined in Section 414(q) of the Code).

- *Equal rights and privileges.* All ESPP participants must enjoy the same rights and privileges under the plan, except that the amount of stock that may be purchased may be based on compensation differences (e.g., a percentage of compensation).

- *Purchase price.* The purchase price may not be less than the lesser of 85% of the fair market value of the stock

(1) at the beginning of the offering period, or (2) on the purchase date.

- *Maximum term.* The maximum term of offering periods under an ESPP may not exceed 27 months unless the purchase price is based solely on the fair market value at the time of purchase, in which case the offering period may be as long as 5 years.

- *$25,000 limit.* Under all ESPPs of the employer company and its parent and subsidiary corporations, an employee may not purchase more than $25,000 worth of stock (determined based on the fair market value on the first day of the offering period) for each calendar year in which the offering period is in effect.

- *Nontransferability.* An employee's right to purchase stock under the ESPP may not be transferred except by will of the laws of descent and distribution and may be exercisable during the employee's life only by the employee.

Designing an ESPP

Within the broad framework of Section 423, there is a good deal of flexibility with regard to plan design.

Number of Shares

There is no limit per se on the number of shares that can be issued under an ESPP. The number of shares reserved under an ESPP should take into account the number of shares available to employees under other stock-based programs, the value of the stock, the duration of the offering, limits on employee contributions, eligibility requirements, and so on. In my experience, it is common for employers to reserve as little as 1% and as much as 8.5% of their outstanding shares for their ESPPs, with an average of about 3.5%. Some employers include an "evergreen" or automatic stock replenishment provision in their ESPP. With such a provision, the number of shares available for issuance under the plan increases automatically, typically each year, based on a specified percentage of the employer's outstanding shares (e.g., 2.5% per year). For tax reasons, the annual increase should be subject to a fixed and determinable limit (e.g., 250,000 shares). An evergreen provision avoids having to continually seek shareholder approval of plan share increases. This can also help the employer avoid a compensation charge for financial accounting purposes if the plan runs out of shares during an offering period. While evergreen provisions are not generally viewed favorably by shareholders, particularly institutional shareholders, approval of such a provision in an ESPP is apparently more palatable to shareholders than an evergreen provision in the employer's stock option plan.

Some employers limit their ESPP share consumption by imposing a cap on the number of shares that can be issued in any one offering period. Such a feature allows employers to plan for future share increases and the associated shareholder approval.

Dilution

Other than the number of shares in the plan, the two factors primarily responsible for the dilutive effect of an ESPP are the purchase price of the stock and the duration of the offering period. As a rule, the longer the offering period, the more dilutive the plan, since employees become more likely to purchase their shares at a substantial discount. For example, assume that the fair market value of the employer's stock on the date of grant is $30, and with a 15% discount, the purchase price would be $25.50 (85% of $30). Assume further that at month 24 the fair market value of the stock is $48. By allowing employees to purchase the shares at 85% of the value on the date of grant (i.e., $25.50), the 15% discount would increase, in this example, to a discount of 47% of the value on the date of purchase. The dilutive effect is even more pronounced in plans that include a feature (discussed in greater detail below) under which participants automatically flip into a new offering period in the event of a decline in the value of the company's stock.

Offering Periods

ESPPs typically permit participants to purchase shares at the end of an "offering period," which typically runs from 3 to 27 months. Most plans have offering periods of either 6 months or some multiple thereof (e.g., 12 months or 24 months).

Plans with offering periods of more than six months typically include interim "purchase periods." For example, if the offering period is 24 months, employees might be allowed to purchase shares at the end of each of the four 6-month purchase periods within the 24-month offering period. In this situation, the purchase price in any one purchase period is usually based on the fair market value on the first day of the offering period or the last day of the particular purchase period, whichever is lower. Plans with offering periods longer than 6 months are more difficult to administer, both because of the interim purchase periods and because of the fact that in most plans of this kind there are overlapping offering periods (e.g., a new 24-month offering commencing every 6 months).

Some ESPPs include an offering period "reset" provision. These plans typically include offering periods that are 12 or 24 months long and begin every 6 months. For example, a 24-month offering period plan might include four 6-month purchase periods (i.e., purchases occur every 6 months during the offering period.) Under a reset provision, if the company's stock declines in value, at the end of a purchase period, the employees are considered to have automatically withdrawn from that offering period and enrolled in the next 24-month offering period. This feature gives the employee the lowest possible purchase price because the purchase price is reset as of the first day of the new offering period.

Some plans offer 12- or 24-month offering periods without interim purchases or otherwise restrict the transferability of purchased shares. These plans preclude employees from selling their shares immediately after purchase, and are intended to foster greater employee stock ownership.

Appendices 1-1 and 1-2 are sample ESPP plan documents providing for 6-month and 24-month offering periods respectively.

Contribution Limits

Section 423 limits purchases under an ESPP to $25,000 worth of stock in any one calendar year, valued as of the first day of the offering period. Under this rule, if a plan has a 12-month offering period beginning each January 1, and the value of the stock on a particular January 1 is $10, then no employee may purchase more than 2,500 shares ($25,000 divided by 10) in that offering period. Where the offering period extends over more than one calendar year, the limit is $25,000 worth of stock for each calendar year in which the offering period is in effect.

Other than this limit, there is no statutory limitation on employee contributions. However, most plans limit employee contributions to a fixed percentage of compensation, generally 10%–15%. For most plan participants, this limit usually falls well below the statutory $25,000 limitation.

Compensation

Closely related to the percentage limitation is the plan definition of compensation. Generally, base pay is the simplest, but another definition can be used if base pay does not accurately reflect the makeup of the employees' compensation.

Eligibility

Almost employees may participate in an ESPP. Section 423 of the Code permits a plan to exclude employees who have been employed for less than two years or who are employed for less than 20 hours per week or five months per year. Also, owners of 5% or more of the common stock of a company by statute are not permitted to participate. Most companies impose either no service requirements or require only a brief employment period to participate, such as three months. Any service requirement should be considered in light of employee turnover, competitive practices, and the eligibility requirements of other company plans.

Offering periods often commence every six months. As a result, new hires may have to wait up to six months to participate in an ESPP, in addition to any service requirement.

Participation by Non-U.S. Employees

Often, employers with employees working outside of the U.S. wish to extend ESPP participation to such employees. Before expanding an ESPP outside the United States, however, employers should become familiar with the applicable laws and regulations of each of the foreign countries where participation will be extended. A discussion of these laws and regulations is beyond the scope of this chapter.

Employers will also need to consider the impact of such participation on qualification of their ESPP under Section 423. Among other things, Section 423 requires (1) that all otherwise eligible employees of any corporation whose employees participate be allowed to participate in the ESPP, and (2) that such participants be allowed to participate on the same terms and conditions. These requirements can be problematic with respect to non-U.S. participants. Local laws sometimes impose requirements that are unique to employees in a particular country, which could violate the equal rights and privileges requirement under Section 423. Similarly, problems can arise where the non-U.S. employees work out of branch offices or divisions, since the non-U.S. employees will be considered employees of the U.S. employer for purposes of Section 423.

As an alternative to adding non-U.S. employees to the ESPP, many employers implement mirror ESPPs for their non-U.S. employees. These plans, which are not intended to qualify under Section 423, give employers more flexibility in designing the plan to meet the particular requirements of each country and with respect to each employee group. Moreover, it preserves the 423 plan for the benefit of U.S. employees who can benefit from the favorable tax treatment offered under tax-qualified plans.

Maximum Number of Shares

In addition to the $25,000 limit discussed above, most plans establish a limit on a number of shares that may be purchased by any one participant in an offering period. This satisfies a rather loose IRS requirement that applies where the number of shares that will be purchased is not known until the last day of the offering period. The IRS takes a position that a plan must establish a maximum cap as of the first day of the offering period. Most plans define the maximum cap with reference to a formula or based on a specific number of shares.

Interest

Money contributed by the plan by employees becomes part of the employer's general assets. In the event the employee terminates employment, this money is refunded, typically without interest. A few employers provide that money returned to employees is credited with interest at some nominal rate, such as 5%.

Federal Income Tax Considerations

Section 423 ESPPs

If a plan meets all the requirements discussed above, an employee who purchases stock under the ESPP will not recognize income for federal income tax purposes on the purchase but will instead defer the tax consequences until the employee sells or otherwise disposes of the stock.

If stock that was purchased under an ESPP is held for *more than* one year after the date of purchase *and* more than two years after the beginning of the offering period, or if the employee dies while owning the shares, a portion of the overall gain will be taxed as ordinary income upon the sale (or other disposition). The amount of ordinary income equals the lesser of (1) the actual gain (the amount by which the market value of the shares on the date of sale, gift or death exceeds the purchase price), or (2) the purchase price discount (however, if the purchase price is not calculable on the first day of the offering period, the purchase price discount is computed as of the first day of the offering period as though the purchase occurred on that day). All additional gain upon the sale of stock is treated as long-term capital gain. If the shares are sold and the sale price is less than the purchase price, there is no ordinary income, and the employee has a long-term capital loss for the difference between the sale price and the purchase price.

If the stock is sold, or is otherwise disposed of, including by way of gift, within either of the Section 423 holding periods (a "disqualifying disposition"), the employee recognizes ordinary income at the time of sale or other disposition taxable to the extent that the fair market value of the stock at the date of purchase was greater than the purchase price (i.e., the "spread" at purchase). This amount is considered ordinary compensation income in the year of sale or other disposition even if no gain is realized on the sale or disposition. This would be the case, for example, in the event of a gift. The difference, if any, between the proceeds of sale and the fair market value of the stock at the date of purchase is a capital gain or loss, which is long-term if the stock has been held more than one year. Ordinary income recognized by the employee upon a disqualifying disposition constitutes taxable income that must generally be reported on a Form W-2. Although the IRS appears to take the position that employers must withhold taxes in this situation, few employers do, in reliance on Rev. Rul. 71-52.

Subject to the limitations of Section 162(m) (the $1,000,000 deduction limit), the employer receives a tax deduction only to the extent that a participant recognizes ordinary income on a disqualifying disposition. The employer does not receive a deduction if the participant meets the holding period requirements. Since the purchase price is typically expressed as a discount from fair market value, compensation recognized by a participant will not be considered "performance-based" within the meaning of Section 162(m), and will therefore apply against the $1,000,000 deduction limitation under that section. To enable the employer to take full advantage of its tax deduction, participants should be required to notify the employer in writing of the date and terms of any disposition of stock purchased under an ESPP.

Section 6039 of the Code requires that the employer provide participants with an information statement by January 31 of the year following the year in which they transfer shares purchased under an ESPP. While penalties may be imposed on an employer who fails to furnish such statements, the IRS has informally indicated that it will not impose such penalties.

Appendix 1-3 illustrates the tax treatment of employees under a Section 423 plan.

Non-Section 423 ESPPs

In some cases, an ESPP may not qualify under Section 423, either by design or as a result of plan operation. In such cases, stock purchased under the plan will be treated, for tax purposes, as though it had been acquired under a nonstatutory stock option. As a result, a plan participant will not recognize income by virtue of participating in the plan, but will recognize ordinary compensation income for federal income tax purposes at the time of purchase, measured by the excess, if any, in the value of the shares at the time of purchase over the purchase price. If the participant is also an employee of the company, the compensation income recognized at the time of purchase will be treated as wages and will be subject to tax withholding by the company. Subject to the deduction limitation under Section 162(m), the company will be entitled to a tax deduction in the amount and at the time that the plan participant recognizes compensation income with respect to shares acquired under the plan, provided the company properly reports the income recognized by the participant (e.g., on Form W-2). Upon a resale of shares by the participant, any difference between the sales price and the purchase price (plus any compensation income recognized with respect to such shares) will be capital gain or loss and will qualify for long-term capital gain or loss treatment if the shares have been held for more than one year. Currently, the tax rate on net capital gain (net long-term capital gain minus net short-term capital loss) is capped at 20%. Capital losses are allowed in full against capital gains and up to $3,000 of other income.

Additional Considerations

Accounting Considerations

For a detailed treatment of the accounting considerations for ESPPs, see the chapter in this book on "Accounting for Employee Stock Purchase Plans."

Shareholder Approval

Section 423 of the Code requires that an ESPP be approved by company shareholders within 12 months of its adoption by the board of directors. No further shareholder approval is required, unless the company amends the plan to increase the number of shares available for issuance or changes the designation of corporations whose employees may participate in the plan (unless the plan provides that such designations may be made from time to time).

Federal Securities Law

For public companies, shares issued under an ESPP are typically registered with the Securities and Exchange Commission (SEC) on Form S-8. Registration of shares by means of Form S-8 is relatively straightforward. Form S-8 consists of two parts, a prospectus and an information statement. The prospectus is intended to be distributed to participants but is not filed with the SEC. The information statement, which must be filed with the SEC, largely consists of documents, such as annual financial reports, that have been prepared by the company for other purposes and are incorporated in the S-8 by reference.

As a result of the 1996 changes to Rule 16b-3 of the Securities and Exchange Act of 1934, ESPP transactions (other than sales of shares purchased under any ESPP) are exempt from Section 16(b) of the Exchange Act (i.e., the short-swing profit rules). Transactions under any ESPP are exempt from the reporting requirements of Section 16(a) as well.

Appendix 1-1:
Sample Plan with Six-Month Offering Periods

MWS Co.
1999 Employee Stock Purchase Plan

1. *Purpose.* The purpose of the Plan is to provide employees of the Company and its Designated Subsidiaries with an opportunity to purchase Common Stock of the Company through accumulated payroll deductions. It is the intention of the Company to have the Plan qualify as an "Employee Stock Purchase Plan" under Section 423 of the Internal Revenue Code of 1986, as amended. The provisions of the Plan, accordingly, shall be construed so as to extend and limit participation in a manner consistent with the requirements of that section of the Code.

2. *Definitions.*

   (a) "Board" shall mean the Board of Directors of the Company.

   (b) "Code" shall mean the Internal Revenue Code of 1986, as amended.

   (c) "Common Stock" shall mean the Common Stock of the Company.

   (d) "Company" shall mean MWS Co., a Delaware corporation, and any Designated Subsidiary of the Company.

   (e) "Compensation" shall mean all base straight time gross earnings and commissions, exclusive of payments for overtime, shift premium, incentive compensation, incentive payments, bonuses and other compensation.

   (f) "Designated Subsidiary" shall mean any Subsidiary which has been designated by the Board from time to time in its sole discretion as eligible to participate in the Plan.

   (g) "Employee" shall mean any individual who is an Employee of the Company for tax purposes whose customary employment with the Company is at least twenty (20) hours per week and more than five (5) months in any calendar year. For purposes of the Plan, the employment relationship shall be treated as continuing intact while the individual is on sick leave or other leave of absence approved by the Company. Where the period of leave exceeds 90 days and the individual's right to reemployment is not guaranteed either by statute or by contract, the employment relationship shall be deemed to have terminated on the 91st day of such leave.

(h) "Enrollment Date" shall mean the first day of each Offering Period.

(i) "Exercise Date" shall mean the last day of each Offering Period.

(j) "Fair Market Value" shall mean, as of any date, the value of Common Stock determined as follows:

(1) If the Common Stock is listed on any established stock exchange or a national market system, including without limitation the Nasdaq National Market or The Nasdaq SmallCap Market of The Nasdaq Stock Market, its Fair Market Value shall be the closing sales price for such stock (or the closing bid, if no sales were reported) as quoted on such exchange or system for the last market trading day on the date of such determination, as reported in *The Wall Street Journal* or such other source as the Board deems reliable, or;

(2) If the Common Stock is regularly quoted by a recognized securities dealer but selling prices are not reported, its Fair Market Value shall be the mean of the closing bid and asked prices for the Common Stock on the date of such determination, as reported in The Wall Street Journal or such other source as the Board deems reliable, or;

(3) In the absence of an established market for the Common Stock, the Fair Market Value thereof shall be determined in good faith by the Board.

(k) "Offering Period" shall mean a period of approximately six (6) months during which an option granted pursuant to the Plan may be exercised, commencing on the first Trading Day on or after [_____] and terminating on the last Trading Day in the period ending the following [_____], or commencing on the first Trading Day on or after [_____] and terminating on the last Trading Day in the period ending the following [_____]; provided, however, that the first Offering Period under the Plan shall commence with the first Trading Day on or after the date on which the Securities and Exchange Commission declares the Company's Registration Statement effective and ending on the last Trading Day on or before [_____]. The duration of Offering Periods may be changed pursuant to Section 4 of this Plan.

(l) "*Plan*" shall mean this Employee Stock Purchase Plan.

(m) "Purchase Price" shall mean an amount equal to 85% of the Fair Market Value of a share of Common Stock on the Enrollment Date or on the Exercise Date, whichever is lower; provided, however, that the Purchase Price may be adjusted by the Board pursuant to Section 20.

(n) "Reserves" shall mean the number of shares of Common Stock covered by each option under the Plan which have not yet been exercised and the number of shares of Common Stock which have been authorized for issuance under the Plan but not yet placed under option.

(o) "Subsidiary" shall mean a corporation, domestic or foreign, of which not less than 50% of the voting shares are held by the Company or a Subsidiary, whether or not such corporation now exists or is hereafter organized or acquired by the Company or a Subsidiary.

(p) "Trading Day" shall mean a day on which national stock exchanges and the Nasdaq System are open for trading.

3. *Eligibility.*

    (a) Any Employee who shall be employed by the Company on a given Enrollment Date shall be eligible to participate in the Plan.

    (b) Any provisions of the Plan to the contrary notwithstanding, no Employee shall be granted an option under the Plan (i) to the extent that, immediately after the grant, such Employee (or any other person whose stock would be attributed to such Employee pursuant to Section 424(d) of the Code) would own capital stock of the Company and/or hold outstanding options to purchase such stock possessing five percent (5%) or more of the total combined voting power or value of all classes of the capital stock of the Company or of any Subsidiary, or (ii) to the extent that his or her rights to purchase stock under all employee stock purchase plans of the Company and its subsidiaries accrues at a rate which exceeds Twenty-Five Thousand Dollars ($25,000) worth of stock (determined at the fair market value of the shares at the time such option is granted) for each calendar year in which such option is outstanding at any time.

4. *Offering Periods.* The Plan shall be implemented by consecutive Offering Periods with a new Offering Period commencing on the first Trading Day on or after [_____] and [_____] each year, or on such other date as the Board shall determine, and continuing thereafter until terminated in accordance with Section 20 hereof; provided, however, that the first Offering Period under the Plan shall commence with the first Trading Day on or after the date on which the Securities and Exchange Commission declares the Company's Registration Statement effective and ending on the last Trading Day on or before [_____]. The Board shall have the power to change the duration of Offering Periods (including the commencement dates thereof) with respect to future offerings without stockholder approval if such change is

announced at least five (5) days prior to the scheduled beginning of the first Offering Period to be affected thereafter.

5. *Participation.*

   (a) An eligible Employee may become a participant in the Plan by completing a subscription agreement authorizing payroll deductions in the form of Exhibit A to this Plan and filing it with the Company's payroll office prior to the applicable Enrollment Date.

   (b) Payroll deductions for a participant shall commence on the first payroll following the Enrollment Date and shall end on the last payroll in the Offering Period to which such authorization is applicable, unless sooner terminated by the participant as provided in Section 10 hereof.

6. *Payroll Deductions.*

   (a) At the time a participant files his or her subscription agreement, he or she shall elect to have payroll deductions made on each pay day during the Offering Period in an amount not exceeding [___] percent (__%) of the Compensation which he or she receives on each pay day during the Offering Period.

   (b) All payroll deductions made for a participant shall be credited to his or her account under the Plan and shall be withheld in whole percentages only. A participant may not make any additional payments into such account.

   (c) A participant may discontinue his or her participation in the Plan as provided in Section 10 hereof, or may increase or decrease the rate of his or her payroll deductions during the Offering Period by completing or filing with the Company a new subscription agreement authorizing a change in payroll deduction rate. The Board may, in its discretion, limit the number of participation rate changes during any Offering Period. The change in rate shall be effective with the first full payroll period following five (5) business days after the Company's receipt of the new subscription agreement unless the Company elects to process a given change in participation more quickly. A participant's subscription agreement shall remain in effect for successive Offering Periods unless terminated as provided in Section 10 hereof.

(d) Notwithstanding the foregoing, to the extent necessary to comply with Section 423(b)(8) of the Code and Section 3(b) hereof, a participant's payroll deductions may be decreased to zero percent (0%) at any time during an Offering Period. Payroll deductions shall recommence at the rate provided in such participant's subscription agreement at the beginning of the first Offering Period which is scheduled to end in the following calendar year, unless terminated by the participant as provided in Section 10 hereof.

(e) At the time the option is exercised, in whole or in part, or at the time some or all of the Company's Common Stock issued under the Plan is disposed of, the participant must make adequate provision for the Company's federal, state, or other tax withholding obligations, if any, which arise upon the exercise of the option or the disposition of the Common Stock. At any time, the Company may, but shall not be obligated to, withhold from the participant's compensation the amount necessary for the Company to meet applicable withholding obligations, including any withholding required to make available to the Company any tax deductions or benefits attributable to sale or early disposition of Common Stock by the Employee.

7. *Grant of Option.* On the Enrollment Date of each Offering Period, each eligible Employee participating in such Offering Period shall be granted an option to purchase on the Exercise Date of such Offering Period (at the applicable Purchase Price) up to a number of shares of the Company's Common Stock determined by dividing such Employee's payroll deductions accumulated prior to such Exercise Date and retained in the Participant's account

as of the Exercise Date by the applicable Purchase Price; provided that in no event shall an Employee be permitted to purchase during each Offering Period more than [_____] shares (subject to any adjustment pursuant to Section 19), and provided further that such purchase shall be subject to the limitations set forth in Sections 3(b) and 12 hereof. Exercise of the option shall occur as provided in Section 8 hereof, unless the participant has withdrawn pursuant to Section 10 hereof. The Option shall expire on the last day of the Offering Period.

8. *Exercise of Option.* Unless a participant withdraws from the Plan as provided in Section 10 hereof, his or her option for the purchase of shares shall be exercised automatically on the Exercise Date, and the maximum number of full shares subject to option shall be purchased for such participant at the applicable Purchase Price with the accumulated payroll deductions in his or her account. No fractional shares shall be purchased; any payroll deductions accumulated in a participant's account which are not sufficient to purchase a full share shall be retained in the participant's account for the subsequent Offering Period, subject to earlier withdrawal by the participant as provided in Section 10 hereof. Any other monies left over in a participant's account after the Exercise Date shall be returned to the participant. During a participant's lifetime, a participant's option to purchase shares hereunder is exercisable only by him or her.

9. *Delivery.* As promptly as practicable after each Exercise Date on which a purchase of shares occurs, the Company shall arrange the delivery to each participant, as appropriate, the shares purchased upon exercise of his or her option.

10. *Withdrawal.*

   (a) A participant may withdraw all but not less than all the payroll deductions credited to his or her account and not yet used to exercise his or her option under the Plan at any time by giving written notice to the Company in the form of Exhibit B to this Plan. All of the participant's payroll deductions credited to his or her account shall be paid to such participant promptly after receipt of notice of withdrawal, and such participant's option for the Offering Period shall be automatically terminated, and no further payroll deductions for the purchase of shares shall be made for such Offering Period. If a participant withdraws from an Offering Period, payroll deductions shall not resume at the beginning of the succeeding Offering Period unless the participant delivers to the Company a new subscription agreement.

(b) A participant's withdrawal from an Offering Period shall not have any effect upon his or her eligibility to participate in any similar plan which may hereafter be adopted by the Company or in succeeding Offering Periods which commence after the termination of the Offering Period from which the participant withdraws.

11. *Termination of Employment.* Upon a participant's ceasing to be an Employee for any reason, he or she shall be deemed to have elected to withdraw from the Plan and the payroll deductions credited to such participant's account during the Offering Period but not yet used to exercise the option shall be returned to such participant or, in the case of his or her death, to the person or persons entitled thereto under Section 15 hereof, and such participant's option shall be automatically terminated. The preceding sentence notwithstanding, a participant who receives payment in lieu of notice of termination of employment shall be treated as continuing to be an Employee for the participant's customary number of hours per week of employment during the period in which the participant is subject to such payment in lieu of notice.

12. *Interest.* No interest shall accrue on the payroll deductions of a participant in the Plan.

13. *Stock.*

(a) Subject to adjustment upon changes in capitalization of the Company as provided in Section 19 hereof, the maximum number of shares of the Company's Common Stock which shall be made available for sale under the Plan shall be [_____ (____)] shares, [plus an annual increase to be added on the first day of the Company's fiscal year beginning in [Year] equal to the lesser of (i) [____] shares, (ii) [____%] of the outstanding shares on such date or (iii) a lesser amount determined by the Board]. If, on a given Exercise Date, the number of shares with respect to which options are to be exercised exceeds the number of shares then available under the Plan, the Company shall make a pro rata allocation of the shares remaining available for purchase in as uniform a manner as shall be practicable and as it shall determine to be equitable.

(b) The participant shall have no interest or voting right in shares covered by his option until such option has been exercised.

(c) Shares to be delivered to a participant under the Plan shall be registered in the name of the participant or in the name of the participant and his or her spouse.

14. *Administration.* The Plan shall be administered by the Board or a committee of members of the Board appointed by the Board. The Board or its committee shall have full and exclusive discretionary authority to construe, interpret and apply the terms of the Plan, to determine eligibility and to adjudicate all disputed claims filed under the Plan. Every finding, decision and determination made by the Board or its committee shall, to the full extent permitted by law, be final and binding upon all parties.

15. *Designation of Beneficiary.*

(a) A participant may file a written designation of a beneficiary who is to receive any shares and cash, if any, from the participant's account under the Plan in the event of such participant's death subsequent to an Exercise Date on which the option is exercised but prior to delivery to such participant of such shares and cash. In addition, a participant may file a written designation of a beneficiary who is to receive any cash from the participant's account under the Plan in the event of such participant's death prior to exercise of the option. If a participant is married and the designated beneficiary is not the spouse, spousal consent shall be required for such designation to be effective.

(b) Such designation of beneficiary may be changed by the participant at any time by written notice. In the event of the death of a participant and in the absence of a beneficiary validly designated under the Plan who is living at the time of such participant's death, the Company shall deliver such shares and/or cash to the executor or administrator of the estate of the participant, or if no such executor or administrator has been appointed (to the knowledge of the Company), the Company, in its discretion, may deliver such shares and/or cash to the spouse or to any one or more dependents or relatives of the participant, or if no spouse, dependent or relative is known to the Company, then to such other person as the Company may designate.

16. *Transferability.* Neither payroll deductions credited to a participant's account nor any rights with regard to the exercise of an option or to receive shares under the Plan may be assigned, transferred, pledged or otherwise disposed of in any way (other than by will, the laws of descent and distribution or as provided in Section 15 hereof) by the participant. Any such attempt at assignment, transfer, pledge or other disposition shall be without effect, except that the Company may treat such act as an election to withdraw funds from an Offering Period in accordance with Section 10 hereof.

17. *Use of Funds.* All payroll deductions received or held by the Company under the Plan may be used by the Company for any corporate purpose, and the Company shall not be obligated to segregate such payroll deductions.

18. *Reports.* Individual accounts shall be maintained for each participant in the Plan. Statements of account shall be

given to participating Employees at least annually, which statements shall set forth the amounts of payroll deductions, the Purchase Price, the number of shares purchased and the remaining cash balance, if any.

19. *Adjustments Upon Changes in Capitalization, Dissolution, Liquidation, Merger or Asset Sale.*

   (a) *Changes in Capitalization.* Subject to any required action by the stockholders of the Company, the Reserves, the maximum number of shares each participant may purchase per Offering Period (pursuant to Section 7), as well as the price per share and the number of shares of Common Stock covered by each option under the Plan which has not yet been exercised shall be proportionately adjusted for any increase or decrease in the number of issued shares of Common Stock resulting from a stock split, reverse stock split, stock dividend, combination or reclassification of the Common Stock, or any other increase or decrease in the number of shares of Common Stock effected without receipt of consideration by the Company; provided, however, that conversion of any convertible securities of the Company shall not be deemed to have been "effected without receipt of consideration". Such adjustment shall be made by the Board, whose determination in that respect shall be final, binding and conclusive. Except as expressly provided herein, no issuance by the Company of shares of stock of any class, or securities convertible into shares of stock of any class, shall affect, and no adjustment by reason thereof shall be made with respect to, the number or price of shares of Common Stock subject to an option.

   (b) *Dissolution or Liquidation.* In the event of the proposed dissolution or liquidation of the Company, the Offering Period then in progress shall be shortened by setting a new Exercise Date (the "New Exercise Date"), and shall terminate immediately prior to the consummation of such proposed dissolution or liquidation, unless provided otherwise by the Board. The

New Exercise Date shall be before the date of the Company's proposed dissolution or liquidation. The Board shall notify each participant in writing, at least ten (10) business days prior to the New Exercise Date, that the Exercise Date for the participant's option has been changed to the New Exercise Date and that the participant's option shall be exercised automatically on the New Exercise Date, unless prior to such date the participant has withdrawn from the Offering Period as provided in Section 10 hereof.

(c) *Merger or Asset Sale.* In the event of a proposed sale of all or substantially all of the assets of the Company, or the merger of the Company with or into another corporation, each outstanding option shall be assumed or an equivalent option substituted by the successor corporation or a Parent or Subsidiary of the successor corporation. In the event that the successor corporation refuses to assume or substitute for the option, the Offering Period then in progress shall be shortened by setting a new Exercise Date (the "New Exercise Date"). The New Exercise Date shall be before the date of the Company's proposed sale or merger. The Board shall notify each participant in writing, at least ten (10) business days prior to the New Exercise Date, that the Exercise Date for the participant's option has been changed to the New Exercise Date and that the participant's option shall be exercised automatically on the New Exercise Date, unless prior to such date the participant has withdrawn from the Offering Period as provided in Section 10 hereof.

20. *Amendment or Termination.*

(a) The Board of Directors of the Company may at any time and for any reason terminate or amend the Plan. Except as provided in Section 19 hereof, no such termination can affect options previously granted, provided that an Offering Period may be terminated by the Board of Directors on any Exercise Date if the Board determines that the termination of the Offering Period or the Plan is in the best interests of the Company and its stockholders. Except as provided in Section 19 and Section 20 hereof, no amendment may make any change in any option theretofore granted which adversely affects the rights of any participant. To the extent necessary to comply with Section 423 of the Code (or any other applicable law, regulation or stock exchange rule), the Company shall obtain shareholder approval in such a manner and to such a degree as required.

(b) Without stockholder consent and without regard to whether any participant rights may be considered to have been "adversely affected," the Board (or its committee) shall be entitled to change the Offering Periods, limit the frequency and/or number of changes in the amount withheld during an Offering Period, establish the exchange ratio applicable to amounts withheld in a currency other than U.S. dollars, permit payroll withholding in excess of the amount designated by a participant in order to adjust for delays or mistakes in the Company's processing of properly completed withholding elections, establish reasonable waiting and adjustment periods and/or accounting and crediting procedures to ensure that amounts applied toward the purchase of Common Stock for each participant properly correspond with amounts withheld from the participant's Compensation, and establish such other limitations or procedures as the Board (or its committee) determines in its sole discretion advisable which are consistent with the Plan.

(c) In the event the Board determines that the ongoing operation of the Plan may result in unfavorable financial accounting consequences, the Board may, in its discretion and, to the extent necessary or desirable, modify or amend the Plan to reduce or eliminate such accounting consequence including, but not limited to:

(1) altering the Purchase Price for any Offering Period including an Offering Period underway at the time of the change in Purchase Price;

(2) shortening any Offering Period so that Offering Period ends on a new Exercise Date, including an Offering Period underway at the time of the Board action; and

(3) allocating shares.

Such modifications or amendments shall not require stockholder approval or the consent of any Plan participants.

21. *Notices.* All notices or other communications by a participant to the Company under or in connection with the Plan shall be deemed to have been duly given when received in the form specified by the Company at the location, or by the person, designated by the Company for the receipt thereof.

22. *Conditions Upon Issuance of Shares.* Shares shall not be issued with respect to an option unless the exercise of such option and the issuance and delivery of such shares pursuant thereto shall comply with all applicable provisions of law, domestic or foreign, including, without limitation, the Securities Act of 1933, as amended, the Securities Exchange Act of 1934, as amended, the rules and regulations promulgated thereunder, and the requirements of any stock exchange upon which the shares may then be listed, and shall be further subject to the approval of counsel for the Company with respect to such compliance.

As a condition to the exercise of an option, the Company may require the person exercising such option to represent and warrant at the time of any such exercise that the shares are being purchased only for investment and without any present intention to sell or distribute such shares if, in the opinion of counsel for the Company, such a representation is required by any of the aforementioned applicable provisions of law.

23. *Term of Plan.* The Plan shall become effective upon the earlier to occur of its adoption by the Board of Directors or its approval by the stockholders of the Company. It shall continue in effect for a term of ten (10) years unless sooner terminated under Section 20 hereof.

Exhibit A: MWS Co. 1999 Employee Stock Purchase Plan Subscription Agreement

_____ Original Application   Enrollment Date: _____

_____ Change in Payroll Deduction Rate

_____ Change of Beneficiary(ies)

1. _____ hereby elects to participate in the MWS Co. 1999 Employee Stock Purchase Plan (the "Employee Stock Purchase Plan") and subscribes to purchase shares of the Company's Common Stock in accordance with this Subscription Agreement and the Employee Stock Purchase Plan.

2. I hereby authorize payroll deductions from each paycheck in the amount of ____% of my Compensation on each payday (from 1 to _____%) during the Offering Period in accordance with the Employee Stock Purchase Plan. (Please note that no fractional percentages are permitted.)

3. I understand that said payroll deductions shall be accumulated for the purchase of shares of Common Stock at the applicable Purchase Price determined in accordance with the Employee Stock Purchase Plan. I understand that if I do not withdraw from an Offering Period, any accumulated payroll deductions will be used to automatically exercise my option.

4. I have received a copy of the complete Employee Stock Purchase Plan. I understand that my participation in the Employee Stock Purchase Plan is in all respects subject to the terms of the Plan. I understand that my ability to exercise the option under this Subscription Agreement is subject to stockholder approval of the Employee Stock Purchase Plan.

5. Shares purchased for me under the Employee Stock Purchase Plan should be issued in the name(s) of (Employee or Employee and Spouse only):

   _____.

6. I understand that if I dispose of any shares received by me pursuant to the Plan within 2 years after the Enroll-

ment Date (the first day of the Offering Period during which I purchased such shares), I will be treated for federal income tax purposes as having received ordinary income at the time of such disposition in an amount equal to the excess of the fair market value of the shares at the time such shares were purchased by me over the price which I paid for the shares. *I hereby agree to notify the Company in writing within 30 days after the date of any disposition of shares, and I will make adequate provision for Federal, state or other tax withholding obligations, if any, which arise upon the disposition of the Common Stock.* The Company may, but will not be obligated to, withhold from my compensation the amount necessary to meet any applicable withholding obligation including any withholding necessary to make available to the Company any tax deductions or benefits attributable to sale or early disposition of Common Stock by me. If I dispose of such shares at any time after the expiration of the 2-year holding period, I understand that I will be treated for federal income tax purposes as having received income only at the time of such disposition, and that such income will be taxed as ordinary income only to the extent of an amount equal to the lesser of (1) the excess of the fair market value of the shares at the time of such disposition over the purchase price which I paid for the shares, or (2) 15% of the fair market value of the shares on the first day of the Offering Period. The remainder of the gain, if any, recognized on such disposition will be taxed as capital gain.

7. I hereby agree to be bound by the terms of the Employee Stock Purchase Plan. The effectiveness of this Subscription Agreement is dependent upon my eligibility to participate in the Employee Stock Purchase Plan.

8. In the event of my death, I hereby designate the following as my beneficiary(ies) to receive all payments and shares due me under the Employee Stock Purchase Plan:

Name: (please print)

_____

(First)   (Middle)   (Last)

Relationship: _____

Address: _____

_____

Employee's Social
Security Number: _____

Employee's Address: _____

_____

_____

I UNDERSTAND THAT THIS SUBSCRIPTION AGREE-
MENT SHALL REMAIN IN EFFECT THROUGHOUT
SUCCESSIVE OFFERING PERIODS UNLESS TERMI-
NATED BY ME.

Dated: _____

_____

Signature of Employee

_____

Spouse's Signature (If beneficiary other than spouse)

Exhibit B: MWS Co. 1999 Employee Stock Purchase Plan Notice of Withdrawal

The undersigned participant in the Offering Period of the MWS Co. 1999 Employee Stock Purchase Plan which began on _____, _____ (the "Enrollment Date") hereby notifies the Company that he or she hereby withdraws from the Offering Period. He or she hereby directs the Company to pay to the undersigned as promptly as practicable all the payroll deductions credited to his or her account with respect to such Offering Period. The undersigned understands and agrees that his or her option for such Offering Period will be automatically terminated. The undersigned understands further that no further payroll deductions will be made for the purchase of shares in the current Offering Period and the undersigned shall be eligible to participate in succeeding Offering Periods only by delivering to the Company a new Subscription Agreement.

Name and Address of Participant: _____

_____

_____

Signature: _____

Date: _____

Appendix 1-2:
Sample Plan with 24-Month Offering Periods

MWS Co.
1999 Employee Stock Purchase Plan

The following constitute the provisions of the 1999 Employee Stock Purchase Plan of MWS Co.

1. *Purpose.* The purpose of the Plan is to provide employees of the Company and its Designated Subsidiaries with an opportunity to purchase Common Stock of the Company through accumulated payroll deductions. It is the intention of the Company to have the Plan qualify as an "Employee Stock Purchase Plan" under Section 423 of the Internal Revenue Code of 1986, as amended. The provisions of the Plan, accordingly, shall be construed so as to extend and limit participation in a manner consistent with the requirements of that section of the Code.

2. *Definitions.*

   (a) "Board" shall mean the Board of Directors of the Company.

   (b) "Code" shall mean the Internal Revenue Code of 1986, as amended.

   (c) "Common Stock" shall mean the common stock of the Company.

   (d) "Company" shall mean MWS Co. and any Designated Subsidiary of the Company.

   [(e) "Compensation" shall mean all base straight time gross earnings and commissions, but exclusive of payments for overtime, shift premium, incentive compensation, incentive payments, bonuses and other compensation.]

   (f) "Designated Subsidiary" shall mean any Subsidiary which has been designated by the Board from time to time in its sole discretion as eligible to participate in the Plan.

(g) "Employee" shall mean any individual who is an Employee of the Company for tax purposes whose customary employment with the Company is at least twenty (20) hours per week and more than five (5) months in any calendar year. For purposes of the Plan, the employment relationship shall be treated as continuing intact while the individual is on sick leave or other leave of absence approved by the Company. Where the period of leave exceeds 90 days and the individual's right to reemployment is not guaranteed either by statute or by contract, the employment relationship shall be deemed to have terminated on the 91st day of such leave.

(h) "Enrollment Date" shall mean the first Trading Day of each Offering Period.

(i) "Exercise Date" shall mean the last Trading Day of each Purchase Period.

(j) "Fair Market Value" shall mean, as of any date, the value of Common Stock determined as follows:

(1) If the Common Stock is listed on any established stock exchange or a national market system, including without limitation the Nasdaq National Market or The Nasdaq SmallCap Market of The Nasdaq Stock Market, its Fair Market Value shall be the closing sales price for such stock (or the closing bid, if no sales were reported) as quoted on such exchange or system for the last market trading day on the date of such determination, as reported in *The Wall Street Journal* or such other source as the Board deems reliable;

(2) If the Common Stock is regularly quoted by a recognized securities dealer but selling prices are not reported, its Fair Market Value shall be the mean of the closing bid and asked prices for the Common Stock on the date of such determination, as reported in *The Wall Street Journal* or such other source as the Board deems reliable;

(3) In the absence of an established market for the Common Stock, the Fair Market Value thereof shall be determined in good faith by the Board; or

(4) For purposes of the Enrollment Date of the first Offering Period under the Plan, the Fair Market Value shall be the initial price to the public as set forth in the final prospectus included within the registration statement in Form S-1 filed with the Securities and Exchange Commission for the initial public offering of the Company's Common Stock (the "Registration Statement").

(k) "Offering Periods" shall mean the periods of approximately twenty-four (24) months during which an option granted pursuant to the Plan may be exercised, commencing on the first Trading Day on or after [_____] and [_____] of each year and terminating on the last Trading Day in the periods ending twenty-four months later; provided, however, that the first Offering Period under the Plan shall commence with the first Trading Day on or after the date on which the Securities and Exchange Commission declares the Company's Registration Statement effective and ending on the last Trading Day on or before [_____]. The duration and timing of Offering Periods may be changed pursuant to Section 4 of this Plan.

(l) "Plan" shall mean this 1999 Employee Stock Purchase Plan.

(m) "Purchase Period" shall mean the approximately six month period commencing after one Exercise Date and ending with the next Exercise Date, except that the first Purchase Period of any Offering Period shall commence on the Enrollment Date and end with the next Exercise Date.

(n) "Purchase Price" shall mean 85% of the Fair Market Value of a share of Common Stock on the Enrollment Date or on the Exercise Date, whichever is lower;

provided however, that the Purchase Price may be adjusted by the Board pursuant to Section 20.

(o) "Reserves" shall mean the number of shares of Common Stock covered by each option under the Plan which have not yet been exercised and the number of shares of Common Stock which have been authorized for issuance under the Plan but not yet placed under option.

(p) "Subsidiary" shall mean a corporation, domestic or foreign, of which not less than 50% of the voting shares are held by the Company or a Subsidiary, whether or not such corporation now exists or is hereafter organized or acquired by the Company or a Subsidiary.

(q) "Trading Day" shall mean a day on which national stock exchanges and the Nasdaq System are open for trading.

3. *Eligibility.*

(a) Any Employee who shall be employed by the Company on a given Enrollment Date shall be eligible to participate in the Plan.

(b) Any provisions of the Plan to the contrary notwithstanding, no Employee shall be granted an option under the Plan (i) to the extent that, immediately after the grant, such Employee (or any other person whose stock would be attributed to such Employee pursuant to Section 424(d) of the Code) would own capital stock of the Company and/or hold outstanding options to purchase such stock possessing five percent (5%) or more of the total combined voting power or value of all classes of the capital stock of the Company or of any Subsidiary, or (ii) to the extent that his or her rights to purchase stock under all employee stock purchase plans of the Company and its subsidiaries accrues at a rate which exceeds Twenty-Five Thousand Dollars ($25,000) worth of stock (determined at the fair market value of the shares at the time such option is granted) for each calendar year in which such option is outstanding at any time.

4. *Offering Periods.* The Plan shall be implemented by consecutive, overlapping Offering Periods with a new Offering Period commencing on the first Trading Day on or after [_____] and [_____] each year, or on such other date as the Board shall determine, and continuing thereafter until terminated in accordance with Section 20 hereof; provided, however, that the first Offering Period under the Plan shall commence with the first Trading Day on or after the date on which the Securities and Exchange Commission declares the Company's Registration Statement effective and ending on the last Trading Day on or before [_____]. The Board shall have the power to change the duration of Offering Periods (including the commencement dates thereof) with respect to future offerings without shareholder approval if such change is announced [at least five (5) days] prior to the scheduled beginning of the first Offering Period to be affected thereafter.

5. *Participation.*

   (a) An eligible Employee may become a participant in the Plan by completing a subscription agreement authorizing payroll deductions in the form of Exhibit A to this Plan and filing it with the Company's payroll office prior to the applicable Enrollment Date.

   (b) Payroll deductions for a participant shall commence on the first payroll following the Enrollment Date and shall end on the last payroll in the Offering Period to which such authorization is applicable, unless sooner terminated by the participant as provided in Section 10 hereof.

6. *Payroll Deductions.*

   (a) At the time a participant files his or her subscription agreement, he or she shall elect to have payroll deductions made on each pay day during the Offering

Period in an amount not exceeding [_____
(___%)] of the Compensation which he or she receives
on each pay day during the Offering Period.

(b) All payroll deductions made for a participant shall
be credited to his or her account under the Plan and
shall be withheld in whole percentages only. A participant may not make any additional payments into
such account.

(c) A participant may discontinue his or her participation in the Plan as provided in Section 10 hereof, or
may increase or decrease the rate of his or her payroll deductions during the Offering Period by completing or filing with the Company a new subscription agreement authorizing a change in payroll
deduction rate. The Board may, in its discretion, limit
the number of participation rate changes during any
Offering Period. The change in rate shall be effective
with the first full payroll period following five (5)
business days after the Company's receipt of the new
subscription agreement unless the Company elects
to process a given change in participation more
quickly. A participant's subscription agreement shall
remain in effect for successive Offering Periods unless terminated as provided in Section 10 hereof.

(d) Notwithstanding the foregoing, to the extent necessary to comply with Section 423(b)(8) of the Code and
Section 3(b) hereof, a participant's payroll deductions
may be decreased to zero percent (0%) at any time
during a Purchase Period. Payroll deductions shall
recommence at the rate provided in such participant's
subscription agreement at the beginning of the first
Purchase Period which is scheduled to end in the
following calendar year, unless terminated by the
participant as provided in Section 10 hereof.

(e) At the time the option is exercised, in whole or in part,
or at the time some or all of the Company's Common
Stock issued under the Plan is disposed of, the participant must make adequate provision for the Company's

federal, state, or other tax withholding obligations, if any, which arise upon the exercise of the option or the disposition of the Common Stock. At any time, the Company may, but shall not be obligated to, withhold from the participant's compensation the amount necessary for the Company to meet applicable withholding obligations, including any withholding required to make available to the Company any tax deductions or benefits attributable to sale or early disposition of Common Stock by the Employee.

7. *Grant of Option.* On the Enrollment Date of each Offering Period, each eligible Employee participating in such Offering Period shall be granted an option to purchase on each Exercise Date during such Offering Period (at the applicable Purchase Price) up to a number of shares of the Company's Common Stock determined by dividing such Employee's payroll deductions accumulated prior to such Exercise Date and retained in the Participant's account as of the Exercise Date by the applicable Purchase Price; provided that in no event shall an Employee be permitted to purchase during each Purchase Period more than [_____] shares of the Company's Common Stock (subject to any adjustment pursuant to Section 19), and provided further that such purchase shall be subject to the limitations set forth in Sections 3(b) and 12 hereof. The Board may, for future Offering Periods, increase or decrease, in its absolute discretion, the maximum number of shares of the Company's Common Stock an Employee may purchase during each Purchase Period of such Offering Period. Exercise of the option shall occur as provided in Section 8 hereof, unless the participant has withdrawn pursuant to Section 10 hereof. The option shall expire on the last day of the Offering Period.

8. *Exercise of Option.*

(a) Unless a participant withdraws from the Plan as provided in Section 10 hereof, his or her option for the purchase of shares shall be exercised automatically on the Exercise Date, and the maximum number of full shares subject to option shall be purchased for such participant at the applicable Purchase Price with the accumulated payroll deductions in his or her account. No fractional shares shall be purchased; any payroll deductions accumulated in a participant's account which are not sufficient to purchase a full share shall be retained in the participant's account for the subsequent Purchase Period or Offering Period, subject to earlier withdrawal by the participant as provided in Section 10 hereof. Any other monies left over in a participant's account after the Exercise Date shall be returned to the participant. During a participant's lifetime, a participant's option to purchase shares hereunder is exercisable only by him or her.

(b) If the Board determines that, on a given Exercise Date, the number of shares with respect to which options are to be exercised may exceed (i) the number of shares of Common Stock that were available for sale under the Plan on the Enrollment Date of the applicable Offering Period, or (ii) the number of shares available for sale under the Plan on such Exercise Date, the Board may in its sole discretion (x) provide that the Company shall make a pro rata allocation of the shares of Common Stock available for purchase on such Enrollment Date or Exercise Date, as applicable, in as uniform a manner as shall be practicable and as it shall determine in its sole discretion to be equitable among all participants exercising options to purchase Common Stock on such Exercise Date, and continue all Offering Periods then in effect, or (y) provide that the Company shall make a pro rata allocation of the shares available for purchase on such Enrollment Date or Exercise Date, as applicable, in as uniform a manner as shall be practicable and as it shall determine in its sole discretion to be equitable among all participants exercising options to purchase Common Stock on such Exercise Date, and terminate any or all Offering Periods then in effect pursuant to Section 20 hereof. The Company may make pro rata allocation of the shares available on the Enrollment Date of any applicable Offering Period pursuant to the preceding sentence, notwithstanding any authorization of additional shares for issuance under the Plan by the Company's shareholders subsequent to such Enrollment Date.

9. *Delivery.* As promptly as practicable after each Exercise Date on which a purchase of shares occurs, the Company shall arrange the delivery to each participant, as appropriate, of a certificate representing the shares purchased upon exercise of his or her option.

10. *Withdrawal.*

   (a) A participant may withdraw all but not less than all the payroll deductions credited to his or her account and not yet used to exercise his or her option under the Plan at any time by giving written notice to the Company in the form of Exhibit B to this Plan. All of the participant's payroll deductions credited to his or her account shall be paid to such participant promptly after receipt of notice of withdrawal and such participant's option for the Offering Period shall be automatically terminated, and no further payroll deductions for the purchase of shares shall be made for such Offering Period. If a participant withdraws from an Offering Period, payroll deductions shall not resume at the beginning of the succeeding Offering Period unless the participant delivers to the Company a new subscription agreement.

   (b) A participant's withdrawal from an Offering Period shall not have any effect upon his or her eligibility to participate in any similar plan which may hereafter be adopted by the Company or in succeeding Offering Periods which commence after the termination of the Offering Period from which the participant withdraws.

11. *Termination of Employment.* Upon a participant's ceasing to be an Employee, for any reason, he or she shall be deemed to have elected to withdraw from the Plan and

the payroll deductions credited to such participant's account during the Offering Period but not yet used to exercise the option shall be returned to such participant or, in the case of his or her death, to the person or persons entitled thereto under Section 15 hereof, and such participant's option shall be automatically terminated. The preceding sentence notwithstanding, a participant who receives payment in lieu of notice of termination of employment shall be treated as continuing to be an Employee for the participant's customary number of hours per week of employment during the period in which the participant is subject to such payment in lieu of notice.

12. *Interest.* No interest shall accrue on the payroll deductions of a participant in the Plan.

13. *Stock.*

(a) Subject to adjustment upon changes in capitalization of the Company as provided in Section 19 hereof, the maximum number of shares of the Company's Common Stock which shall be made available for sale under the Plan shall be [_____ (_____)] shares, [plus an annual increase to be added on the first day of the Company's fiscal year beginning in [Year] equal to the lesser of (i) [____] shares, (ii) [____%] of the outstanding shares on such date or (iii) a lesser amount determined by the Board] .

(b) The participant shall have no interest or voting right in shares covered by his option until such option has been exercised.

(c) Shares to be delivered to a participant under the Plan shall be registered in the name of the participant or in the name of the participant and his or her spouse.

14. *Administration.* The Plan shall be administered by the Board or a committee of members of the Board appointed by the Board. The Board or its committee shall have full and exclusive discretionary authority to construe, inter-

pret and apply the terms of the Plan, to determine eligibility and to adjudicate all disputed claims filed under the Plan. Every finding, decision and determination made by the Board or its committee shall, to the full extent permitted by law, be final and binding upon all parties.

15. *Designation of Beneficiary.*

   (a) A participant may file a written designation of a beneficiary who is to receive any shares and cash, if any, from the participant's account under the Plan in the event of such participant's death subsequent to an Exercise Date on which the option is exercised but prior to delivery to such participant of such shares and cash. In addition, a participant may file a written designation of a beneficiary who is to receive any cash from the participant's account under the Plan in the event of such participant's death prior to exercise of the option. If a participant is married and the designated beneficiary is not the spouse, spousal consent shall be required for such designation to be effective.

   (b) Such designation of beneficiary may be changed by the participant at any time by written notice. In the event of the death of a participant and in the absence of a beneficiary validly designated under the Plan who is living at the time of such participant's death, the Company shall deliver such shares and/or cash to the executor or administrator of the estate of the participant, or if no such executor or administrator has been appointed (to the knowledge of the Company), the Company, in its discretion, may deliver such shares and/or cash to the spouse or to any one or more dependents or relatives of the participant, or if no spouse, dependent or relative is known to the Company, then to such other person as the Company may designate.

16. *Transferability.* Neither payroll deductions credited to a participant's account nor any rights with regard to the exercise of an option or to receive shares under the Plan

may be assigned, transferred, pledged or otherwise disposed of in any way (other than by will, the laws of descent and distribution or as provided in Section 15 hereof) by the participant. Any such attempt at assignment, transfer, pledge or other disposition shall be without effect, except that the Company may treat such act as an election to withdraw funds from an Offering Period in accordance with Section 10 hereof.

17. *Use of Funds.* All payroll deductions received or held by the Company under the Plan may be used by the Company for any corporate purpose, and the Company shall not be obligated to segregate such payroll deductions.

18. *Reports.* Individual accounts shall be maintained for each participant in the Plan. Statements of account shall be given to participating Employees at least annually, which statements shall set forth the amounts of payroll deductions, the Purchase Price, the number of shares purchased and the remaining cash balance, if any.

19. *Adjustments Upon Changes in Capitalization, Dissolution, Liquidation, Merger or Asset Sale.*

   (a) *Changes in Capitalization.* Subject to any required action by the shareholders of the Company, the Reserves, the maximum number of shares each participant may purchase each Purchase Period (pursuant to Section 7), as well as the price per share and the number of shares of Common Stock covered by each option under the Plan which has not yet been exercised shall be proportionately adjusted for any increase or decrease in the number of issued shares of Common Stock resulting from a stock split, reverse stock split, stock dividend, combination or reclassification of the Common Stock, or any other increase or decrease in the number of shares of Common Stock effected without receipt of consideration by the Company; provided, however, that conversion of any convertible securities of the Company shall not be deemed to have been "effected without receipt of consideration". Such adjustment shall be made by the

Board, whose determination in that respect shall be final, binding and conclusive. Except as expressly provided herein, no issuance by the Company of shares of stock of any class, or securities convertible into shares of stock of any class, shall affect, and no adjustment by reason thereof shall be made with respect to, the number or price of shares of Common Stock subject to an option.

(b) *Dissolution or Liquidation.* In the event of the proposed dissolution or liquidation of the Company, the Offering Period then in progress shall be shortened by setting a new Exercise Date (the "New Exercise Date"), and shall terminate immediately prior to the consummation of such proposed dissolution or liquidation, unless provided otherwise by the Board. The New Exercise Date shall be before the date of the Company's proposed dissolution or liquidation. The Board shall notify each participant in writing, at least ten (10) business days prior to the New Exercise Date, that the Exercise Date for the participant's option has been changed to the New Exercise Date and that the participant's option shall be exercised automatically on the New Exercise Date, unless prior to such date the participant has withdrawn from the Offering Period as provided in Section 10 hereof.

(c) *Merger or Asset Sale.* In the event of a proposed sale of all or substantially all of the assets of the Company, or the merger of the Company with or into another corporation, each outstanding option shall be assumed or an equivalent option substituted by the successor corporation or a Parent or Subsidiary of the successor corporation. In the event that the successor corporation refuses to assume or substitute for the option, any Purchase Periods then in progress shall be shortened by setting a new Exercise Date (the "New Exercise Date") and any Offering Periods then in progress shall end on the New Exercise Date. The New Exercise Date shall be before the date of the Company's proposed sale or merger. The Board shall notify each participant in writing, at least ten (10) business days prior to the New Exercise Date, that the Exercise Date for the participant's option has been changed to the New Exercise Date and that the participant's option shall be exercised automatically on the New Exercise Date, unless prior to such date the participant has withdrawn from the Offering Period as provided in Section 10 hereof.

20. *Amendment or Termination.*

(a) The Board of Directors of the Company may at any time and for any reason terminate or amend the Plan. Except as provided in Section 19 hereof, no such termination can affect options previously granted, provided that an Offering Period may be terminated by the Board of Directors on any Exercise Date if the Board determines that the termination of the Offering Period or the Plan is in the best interests of the Company and its shareholders. Except as provided in Section 19 and this Section 20 hereof, no amendment may make any change in any option theretofore granted which adversely affects the rights of any participant. To the extent necessary to comply with Section 423 of the Code (or any successor rule or provision or any other applicable law, regulation or stock exchange rule), the Company shall obtain shareholder approval in such a manner and to such a degree as required.

(b) Without shareholder consent and without regard to whether any participant rights may be considered to have been "adversely affected," the Board (or its committee) shall be entitled to change the Offering Periods, limit the frequency and/or number of changes in the amount withheld during an Offering Period, establish the exchange ratio applicable to amounts withheld in a currency other than U.S. dollars, permit payroll withholding in excess of the amount designated by a participant in order to adjust for delays or mistakes in the Company's processing of properly completed withholding elections, establish reasonable waiting and adjustment periods and/or accounting and crediting procedures to ensure that amounts applied toward the purchase of Common Stock for each participant properly correspond with amounts withheld from the participant's Compensation, and establish such other limitations or procedures as the Board (or its committee) determines in its sole discretion advisable which are consistent with the Plan.

(c) In the event the Board determines that the ongoing operation of the Plan may result in unfavorable financial accounting consequences, the Board may, in its discretion and, to the extent necessary or desirable, modify or amend the Plan to reduce or eliminate such accounting consequence including, but not limited to:

(1) altering the Purchase Price for any Offering Period including an Offering Period underway at the time of the change in Purchase Price;

(2) shortening any Offering Period so that Offering Period ends on a new Exercise Date, including an Offering Period underway at the time of the Board action; and

(3) allocating shares.

Such modifications or amendments shall not require stockholder approval or the consent of any Plan participants.

21. *Notices.* All notices or other communications by a participant to the Company under or in connection with the Plan shall be deemed to have been duly given when received in the form specified by the Company at the location, or by the person, designated by the Company for the receipt thereof.

22. *Conditions Upon Issuance of Shares.* Shares shall not be issued with respect to an option unless the exercise of such option and the issuance and delivery of such shares pursuant thereto shall comply with all applicable provi-

sions of law, domestic or foreign, including, without limitation, the Securities Act of 1933, as amended, the Securities Exchange Act of 1934, as amended, the rules and regulations promulgated thereunder, and the requirements of any stock exchange upon which the shares may then be listed, and shall be further subject to the approval of counsel for the Company with respect to such compliance.

As a condition to the exercise of an option, the Company may require the person exercising such option to represent and warrant at the time of any such exercise that the shares are being purchased only for investment and without any present intention to sell or distribute such shares if, in the opinion of counsel for the Company, such a representation is required by any of the aforementioned applicable provisions of law.

23. *Term of Plan.* The Plan shall become effective upon the earlier to occur of its adoption by the Board of Directors or its approval by the shareholders of the Company. It shall continue in effect for a term of ten (10) years unless sooner terminated under Section 20 hereof.

24. *Automatic Transfer to Low Price Offering Period.* To the extent permitted by any applicable laws, regulations, or stock exchange rules if the Fair Market Value of the Common Stock on any Exercise Date in an Offering Period is lower than the Fair Market Value of the Common Stock on the Enrollment Date of such Offering Period, then all participants in such Offering Period shall be automatically withdrawn from such Offering Period immediately after the exercise of their option on such Exercise Date and automatically re-enrolled in the immediately following Offering Period as of the first day thereof.

Exhibit A: MWS Co. 1999 Employee Stock Purchase Plan Subscription Agreement

_____ Original Application   Enrollment Date: _____

_____ Change in Payroll Deduction Rate

_____ Change of Beneficiary(ies)

1. _____ hereby elects to participate in the MWS Co. 1999 Employee Stock Purchase Plan (the "Employee Stock Purchase Plan") and subscribes to purchase shares of the Company's Common Stock in accordance with this Subscription Agreement and the Employee Stock Purchase Plan.

2. I hereby authorize payroll deductions from each paycheck in the amount of ____% of my Compensation on each payday (from 1 to ____%) during the Offering Period in accordance with the Employee Stock Purchase Plan. (Please note that no fractional percentages are permitted.)

3. I understand that said payroll deductions shall be accumulated for the purchase of shares of Common Stock at the applicable Purchase Price determined in accordance with the Employee Stock Purchase Plan. I understand that if I do not withdraw from an Offering Period, any accumulated payroll deductions will be used to automatically exercise my option.

4. I have received a copy of the complete Employee Stock Purchase Plan. I understand that my participation in the Employee Stock Purchase Plan is in all respects subject to the terms of the Plan. I understand that my ability to exercise the option under this Subscription Agreement is subject to shareholder approval of the Employee Stock Purchase Plan.

5. Shares purchased for me under the Employee Stock Purchase Plan should be issued in the name(s) of (Employee or Employee and Spouse only):

   _____.

6. I understand that if I dispose of any shares received by me pursuant to the Plan within 2 years after the Enroll-

ment Date (the first day of the Offering Period during which I purchased such shares) or one year after the Exercise Date, I will be treated for federal income tax purposes as having received ordinary income at the time of such disposition in an amount equal to the excess of the fair market value of the shares at the time such shares were purchased by me over the price which I paid for the shares. *I hereby agree to notify the Company in writing within 30 days after the date of any disposition of my shares, and I will make adequate provision for Federal, state or other tax withholding obligations, if any, which arise upon the disposition of the Common Stock.* The Company may, but will not be obligated to, withhold from my compensation the amount necessary to meet any applicable withholding obligation including any withholding necessary to make available to the Company any tax deductions or benefits attributable to sale or early disposition of Common Stock by me. If I dispose of such shares at any time after the expiration of the 2-year and 1-year holding periods, I understand that I will be treated for federal income tax purposes as having received income only at the time of such disposition, and that such income will be taxed as ordinary income only to the extent of an amount equal to the lesser of (1) the excess of the fair market value of the shares at the time of such disposition over the purchase price which I paid for the shares, or (2) 15% of the fair market value of the shares on the first day of the Offering Period. The remainder of the gain, if any, recognized on such disposition will be taxed as capital gain.

7. I hereby agree to be bound by the terms of the Employee Stock Purchase Plan. The effectiveness of this Subscription Agreement is dependent upon my eligibility to participate in the Employee Stock Purchase Plan.

8. In the event of my death, I hereby designate the following as my beneficiary(ies) to receive all payments and shares due me under the Employee Stock Purchase Plan:

Name: (please print)

_____

(First)   (Middle)   (Last)

Relationship: _____

Address: _____

_____

Employee's Social
Security Number: _____

Employee's Address: _____

_____

_____

I UNDERSTAND THAT THIS SUBSCRIPTION AGREE-
MENT SHALL REMAIN IN EFFECT THROUGHOUT
SUCCESSIVE OFFERING PERIODS UNLESS TERMI-
NATED BY ME.

Dated: _____

_____

Signature of Employee

_____

Spouse's Signature (If beneficiary other than spouse)

Exhibit B: MWS Co. 1999 Employee Stock Purchase Plan Notice of Withdrawal

The undersigned participant in the Offering Period of the MWS Co. 1999 Employee Stock Purchase Plan which began on _____, _____ (the "Enrollment Date") hereby notifies the Company that he or she hereby withdraws from the Offering Period. He or she hereby directs the Company to pay to the undersigned as promptly as practicable all the payroll deductions credited to his or her account with respect to such Offering Period. The undersigned understands and agrees that his or her option for such Offering Period will be automatically terminated. The undersigned understands further that no further payroll deductions will be made for the purchase of shares in the current Offering Period and the undersigned shall be eligible to participate in succeeding Offering Periods only by delivering to the Company a new Subscription Agreement.

Name and Address of Participant: _____

_____

_____

Signature: _____

Date: _____

Appendix 1-3:
Illustrations of Tax Treatment Under a
Section 423 ESPP

The following examples illustrate the federal income tax consequences to employees when a participant sells stock purchased under a Section 423 ESPP, and the purchase price is 85% of the lower of (1) the market value on the enrollment date or (2) the market value on the purchase date.

Example 1—Qualifying Disposition The participant sells stock one or more years after the purchase date and two or more years after the enrollment date (i.e., a "qualifying disposition"). The tax consequences at a variety of sale prices are shown below:

Assumptions:

Enrollment date market value	$ 5.00	$ 5.00	$ 5.00	$ 5.00	$ 5.00	$ 5.00
Purchase date market value	10.00	10.00	10.00	4.00	4.00	4.00
Purchase price	4.25	4.25	4.25	3.40	3.40	3.40
Sale price	12.00	8.00	2.50	10.00	3.75	3.00
Actual gain (loss)	$ 7.75	$ 3.75	$(1.75)	$ 6.60	$ .35	$ (.40)

Tax Consequences:

Ordinary income (the lesser of (1) the 15% discount at the enrollment date or (2) the sale price minus the purchase price)	$ .75	$ .75	–	$ .75	$ .35	–
Long-term capital gain (or loss) (sale price, minus ordinary income, minus purchase price)	$7.00	$3.00	$(1.75)	$5.85	–	$ (.40)

Example 2—Disqualifying Disposition   The participant sells
stock within one year after the purchase date or within two
years after the enrollment date (i.e., a "disqualifying disposition"). The tax consequences at a variety of sale prices are
shown below.

Assumptions:

Enrollment date market value	$ 5.00	$ 5.00	$ 5.00	$ 5.00	$ 5.00	$ 5.00
Purchase date market value	10.00	10.00	10.00	4.00	4.00	4.00
Purchase price	4.25	4.25	4.25	3.40	3.40	3.40
Sale price	12.00	8.00	2.50	10.00	3.75	3.00
Actual gain (loss)	$ 7.75	$ 3.75	$(1.75)	$ 6.60	$ .35	$ (.40)

Tax Consequences:

Ordinary income (market value on date of purchase minus purchase price)	$ 5.75	$ 5.75	$ 5.75	$ .60	$ .60	$ .60
Capital gain (or loss)* (sale price, minus ordinary income, minus purchase price)	$2.00	$(2.00)	$(7.50)	$6.00	$ (.25)	$(1.00)

*If shares are held for more than one year, the capital gain or loss is long-term.

CHAPTER 2

Administering an Employee Stock Purchase Plan

Barbara A. Baksa

An employee stock purchase plan (ESPP) provides eligible employees with the opportunity to purchase shares of the company's stock at certain predetermined intervals. Shares are usually purchased at a discount, and the purchase price for the shares is typically paid in the form of payroll deductions authorized by the employee. In addition to the economic benefits provided by this type of plan, the purchase can qualify for preferential tax treatment if the plan meets the requirements of Section 423 of the Internal Revenue Code (the "Code"). Participation in the plan is usually offered to substantially all of the employees of the company.

An ESPP can be an important and advantageous addition to the benefits a company offers to its employees. The plan offers economic and tax advantages to employees and can benefit the company through enhanced employee performance and job satisfaction. But, as with any plan that involves issuing stock to employees, an ESPP can be challenging to administer. The plan must comply with tax and securities regulations as well as adhere to proper accounting standards. Compensation involving stock often seems complex to employees and can require more participation from employees than cash compensation. Since individuals from different departments within the company have a role in the operation of the plan, cooperation with each other and with the company's outside vendors is essential to ensure that the plan operates efficiently. As a result, there are many administrative matters and procedures to be considered and resolved before implementing an ESPP.

This chapter discusses many of the administrative concerns involved in an ESPP, starting with drafting the plan document. The plan implementation process is described, from presenting the plan to employees to the purchase and its aftermath. The discussion is in general terms and is meant to provide guidance only. Each company should feel free to tailor the advice and guidance offered here to its own situation and plan.

Establishing a Plan

A company implementing an ESPP generally establishes a written plan detailing the terms and conditions of the program. A written plan is required if the ESPP is to qualify for the preferential tax treatment available under Section 423. Even where this qualification is not desired, it is advisable to formulate a written plan before implementing the program. Without a written plan, administering an ESPP can be considerably more complex.

The plan may be designed by human resources/benefits personnel in consultation with the company's legal counsel, accountants, and outside compensation or benefits specialists. The individuals responsible for administering the plan should also have input into the plan's design. The objective of the company, the benefit to the proposed participants, cost to the company and to participants, potential liquidity for participants, and the income tax and financial accounting consequences arising from the operation of the plan are all factors that should be taken into consideration in designing the plan.

The company's legal counsel usually prepares the actual plan documents. Once management approves the plan, it is presented to the company's board of directors for consideration and adoption. Since under the corporate laws of most states, the board has authority for all issuances of the company's stock, board approval is generally required before the implementation of an ESPP.

Following adoption by the board of directors, the company usually submits the plan to shareholders for approval. Shareholder approval is necessary for the plan to qualify for preferential tax treatment, and even where this treatment is not desired, shareholder approval might be required by the laws of the state where the company is incorporated, the company's own bylaws, or the exchange on which the company's stock is traded. Even though shareholder approval might not be required, in today's environment it is often advisable to seek shareholder approval to maintain good relations with the company's shareholders.

It is not necessary to submit an ESPP to the Internal Revenue Service (IRS) for approval before the plan is implemented by the company. This is true even if the plan is intended to qualify for preferential tax treatment under Section 423. Occasionally, companies submit a plan to the IRS for review to ensure that the desired preferential tax treatment is available to the participants in the plan, but there may be fees and delays associated with obtaining this approval.

It may be necessary to register the plan with the Securities and Exchange Commission (SEC). Generally, under the federal securities laws, a company may not offer or sell securities pursuant to an ESPP unless the proposed transactions have been registered with the SEC or an exemption from registration is available. If relying upon a suitable exemption, it is not necessary to register with the SEC before the ESPP is implemented. In the case of a company that is subject to the reporting requirements of the Securities Exchange Act of 1934, because there are no exemptions that are suitable to a broad-based employee stock program and to ensure liquidity for plan participants, it is customary to register the plan with the SEC before making offers and sales of securities under the plan.

Generally, publicly traded companies register the shares of stock to be offered pursuant to their ESPPs on Form S-8, a simplified registration statement available exclusively for the employee benefit plans of companies that are subject to the reporting requirements of the Securities Exchange Act of 1934. Form S-8 reflects an abbreviated disclosure format and incorporates by reference information contained in the company's other publicly available documents. Shares of stock acquired under an ESPP registered on Form S-8 are not considered "restricted securities" and generally can be more easily resold by employees.

Most states follow the pattern of the federal securities law and treat ESPPs as involving an offer and sale of securities that must either be registered under state law or exempt from registration. Thus, it may be necessary for a company to register its ESPP in each state in which employees have enrolled to participate in the plan or to locate suitable exemptions. Many states have specific exemptions from registration that cover the offer and sale of securities pursuant to an employee benefit plan, such as an ESPP. These exemptions may impose specific (and often minor) filing requirements on the company.

Both under state and federal law, however, even companies not subject to registration requirements still have to comply with anti-fraud disclosure rules. These will require varying levels of financial disclosure to all employees who are being offered stock.

Plan Provisions, Policies, and Procedures

Many companies establish formal policies and procedures to facilitate the efficient administration of their ESPP. Formal policies enhance the plan administrator's ability to operate the plan consistently with the company's objectives and enable the plan administrator to resolve problems that arise during the course of operating the plan.

The policies discussed in this chapter are often addressed in the company's plan. When developing company policies, it is always a good idea to review the plan document to ensure that these policies are in accordance with its provisions.

Just as when designing a plan, company policies should consider the company's objectives, benefits to the participants, costs to the company and to participants, potential liquidity for participants, and the income tax and financial accounting consequences arising from the operation of the plan.

Who Can Participate

If the plan is intended to qualify for preferential tax treatment, substantially all full-time employees must be allowed to participate. A company can exclude part-time employees (employees that work less than 20 hours per week or less than five months per calendar year), require that the employee meet a minimum service requirement (up to two years), or exclude highly compensated employees without jeopardizing the tax status of the plan. Under no circumstances can an individual owning 5% or more of the company's outstanding stock be allowed to participate in the plan if the plan is intended to qualify for preferential tax treatment under Section 423.

Where a company has a high rate of turnover, it might be desirable to have some minimum service requirement to eliminate some of the administrative burden associated with enrolling and later withdrawing participants from the plan. However, many companies do not have minimum service requirements, and where companies do institute this type of requirement, it is often substantially shorter than two years. The minimum service requirement should probably not be so lengthy that it prevents a majority of employees from participating.

Whether or not part-time employees are allowed to participate probably depends on the number of part-time positions held by employees and the importance of those part-time positions to the overall success of the company. A large, nationwide retail establishment that employs a large number of part-time employees might feel that it is worthwhile for these individuals to participate in the ESPP and that the plan gives the company a competitive edge in the hiring process. On the other hand, a company that merely employs a handful of part-time employees during the summer months might not feel that it is beneficial for these employees to participate in the ESPP.

Contributing Funds

There are various methods that participants can use to contribute funds to an ESPP. The most common method of contribution is through payroll deductions from participants' compensation. Some plans also allow participants to make cash payments to the plan.

Where funds are contributed through payroll deductions, the company must define the type of compensation eligible for contribution to the plan. At a minimum, participants usually contribute from their base salary, but overtime pay, bonuses, commissions and other sources of compensation might also be eligible for contribution to the plan. Many companies permit employees to contribute only whole percentages of compensation. It might also be advisable to require that once an employee has elected to participate in the plan, he or she must contribute at least a minimal amount of funds, such as five to ten dollars per pay period.

From time to time, participants can adjust their level of participation in the plan by either increasing or decreasing their rate of contribution to the plan. Since many companies require that funds contributed to the plan be in the form of payroll deductions, this generally involves a modification to the percentage of compensation that the employee has elected to contribute to the plan. The adjustment is submitted to the payroll department and is reflected in the payroll system. For administrative purposes, it is advisable to establish limits on when and how often adjustments can be made. It may also be necessary to establish employee expectations regarding when these adjustments will be implemented.

A generous policy will allow participants to increase or decrease their rate of contribution at any point and will allow multiple adjustments between purchases, but this generosity may create an undue administrative burden on the payroll department. If there are no restrictions whatsoever on the participants' ability to increase or decrease their rate of contribution, the payroll department could spend an inordinate amount of time completing the paperwork and entries involved in implementing these adjustments. This ultimately is expensive to the company. It is reasonable and appropriate for the company to limit when and how often participants can adjust their rate of contribution. It is not necessary to have the same policy for both increases and decreases. A policy could allow adjustments to decrease at any point, to become effective immediately, but might only allow adjustments to increase only at the start of each purchase period. While easing the administration involved in the plan, however, a policy that is too restrictive might discourage participation in the plan. The company should strive to create a policy that is administratively feasible for the payroll department but which doesn't discourage employees from participating.

If participants are allowed to reduce their contribution levels, it also is necessary to establish whether or not participants may cease contributing to the plan without formally withdrawing from the plan.

Purchase Dates

When establishing an ESPP, the timing of the purchase dates can be a crucial detail. Administering an ESPP usually involves several months of inactivity followed by a few weeks of frantic activity to prepare and complete the purchase. Ideally, the purchase dates are scheduled so that these few weeks of activity do not occur at quarter or year-end, or at other times during which the plan administrator is likely to be busy with other projects.

Publicly traded companies, as part of their insider trading compliance program, frequently establish periods when employee trading is restricted. These periods, referred to as black-out or window periods, are often predictable in that they correspond with earnings releases. Ideally, the purchase dates are scheduled to occur during periods when trading is not restricted. While a purchase of stock pursuant to an ESPP is not typically subject to trading restrictions, sales of stock acquired through this plan often are subject to these restrictions. If the purchase date occurs during one of these restricted periods, employees are not able to sell the shares they have acquired until some time after the purchase date.

Terminating Participation in the Plan

ESPPs are instituted to provide a benefit to employees of the company. Because the plan is intended to benefit employees, individuals that terminate their employment relationship with the company are generally not permitted to participate in the plan. Any funds contributed to the plan that have not been used to purchase shares of stock before the employee's termination are refunded to the participant, typically without interest.

Former employees can be permitted to participate in the plan, although it would be very unusual to allow participation past the first purchase that occurs after the employee's termination. If funds must be contributed in the form of payroll deductions, a terminated employee will not be able to contribute any additional funds to the plan. Purchases by former employees that occur more than three months after the employees' termination dates are not eligible for the preferential tax treatment afforded under Section 423.

Most plans permit employees to withdraw from participation in the plan before the purchase date. The company should define when employees are permitted to withdraw and how soon after withdrawing employees can resume participation in the plan. Generally, employees are required to wait at least until the next entry date, but some companies may require employees to wait a longer period of time. Any contributions refunded to the employee as a result of the withdrawal are typically refunded without interest.

Share Issuance and Sales

There are three methods of issuing shares purchased through an ESPP. Certificates for the purchased shares can be issued and registered in participant names, the purchased shares can be deposited into participants' brokerage accounts, or the participants can arrange to have the shares automatically sold after the purchase occurs (sometimes referred to as a "same-day sale"). There is no requirement that all three of these issuance methods be offered to participants.

If participants do not want to automatically sell the shares they have purchased, there are several benefits to depositing the purchased shares into participants' brokerage accounts instead of issuing certificates registered in the participants' names. Issuing certificates registered in the participants' names causes one certificate to be issued to each participant. Each certificate is delivered separately to each participant, and depending on the delivery service used, there can be either delays or expense associated with this process. Participants assume liability for lost or stolen certificates, and there are additional expenses and delays associated with replacing certificates. Shares deposited in brokerage accounts are registered in the name of the brokerage firm and held by the firm, reducing the participants' liability and the risk that the certificate will be damaged or misplaced. When participants eventually sell their shares, the sale is more efficiently executed if the shares are already deposited in their brokerage accounts.

When participants in the plan are permitted to engage in an automatic sale or can arrange to have their shares deposited into a brokerage account, many companies establish a relationship with one specific brokerage firm (a "designated" or "captive" broker). Participants are required to open an account at this brokerage firm, and their shares are deposited into or sold through this account. Companies that do not want to restrict participants to one firm might establish relationships with two or three firms so that participants have a choice in firms. By asking participants to use a specific brokerage firm, the company ensures that the shares issued as a result of the purchase are all registered in the name of one brokerage firm. This allows the company to complete one combined issuance for all the shares purchased, rather than issuing a separate certificate for each participant, and can result in a significant cost savings. The issuance is usually accomplished electronically, further reducing any expense and delays. The company can also ask that the brokerage firm assist in tracking dispositions (discussed later in this chapter) from participants' accounts. The brokerage firm may offer reduced fees to the plan participants, and some firms can even offer interactive voice response or online systems that give participants direct access to their accounts.

Companies often establish an ESPP to encourage stock ownership among employees. Allowing employees to automatically sell the shares they have purchased through the plan conflicts with this objective. Some companies do not allow participants to automatically sell their purchased shares, and a few companies restrict participants' ability to sell the purchased shares for a period of time following the purchase. Many employees are uncomfortable with market risk, however, and automatically sell their purchased shares to limit their exposure to this risk. While encouraging ownership, not offering an automatic sale program might cause employees to feel that the plan offers less of a benefit to them. Restricting employees' ability to sell for a period of time after the purchase might discourage some employees from participating in the plan altogether. Given these considerations, companies implementing an ESPP should carefully consider the advantages and disadvantages of offering an automatic sale program to their plan participants.

Internal Plan Administration

A successful ESPP requires a partnership among several different individuals and departments. The human resources, payroll, accounting, finance, and legal departments may share various roles in the operation of the plan. In addition, cooperation is required from the company's external payroll provider, transfer agent, and designated brokerage firm. One individual, or a team of individuals, within the company should have responsibility for the plan. This individual or team is responsible for overseeing the operation of the plan. This includes ensuring that the appropriate information about the plan is communicated to employees, collecting and verifying the required information about employee contributions and participation in the plan, determining the number of shares each employee can purchase, verifying that these shares are issued correctly, and communicating the results of the purchase to the transfer agent, designated brokerage firm, accounting and/or finance departments, payroll department, and management.

In companies that already have an established stock administrator, this person may be given responsibility for the ESPP as well. In companies that do not have a stock administrator or where the stock administrator is unable to assume responsibility for the plan, an individual in the human resources department or in the payroll department is typically given responsibility for the ESPP. It is also possible to contract with an external service provider for administration of the plan. Throughout this chapter, the individual responsible for overseeing the ESPP is referred to as the stock administrator.

The individual or team responsible for overseeing the plan will require a method of tracking employee participation and contributions. This might be a spreadsheet, a database, or a software program. It will ultimately be used to determine the number of shares each employee can purchase and to facilitate communicating information about the purchase to the transfer agent, designated brokerage firm, payroll department, accounting and/or finance departments, and management. Spreadsheets and databases can be inexpensive but complicated to create, and it may be difficult to build in the functionality required to truly automate administration of the plan. There are software programs specifically designed to automate administration of ESPPs. Purchasing a software program may represent a greater initial investment, but could ultimately provide savings through greater efficiency and by preventing errors from occurring.

Employee Communication

Employee communication is a key component in the success of any ESPP. Employees who understand the benefits of participating in an ESPP will probably be much more excited about their opportunity to participate in the plan. While the benefits of participation may seem obvious to management, many employees may be unfamiliar with the stock market and may be uncomfortable with the idea of buying stock. This type of plan can seem very complex to employees that have not had an opportunity to participate in an ESPP before and are unfamiliar with the stock market.

An ideal employee communication program includes a variety of formats. At a minimum, written materials describing the plan, or a copy of the plan, are usually provided to all participants. Since the actual plan document is often very detailed and formal, it can be helpful to provide participants with a summary of the plan. This summary can be provided in addition to or in place of the plan itself. Along with the plan summary, it might be beneficial to provide a document of frequently asked questions, in which typical employee questions are answered. These written materials are usually distributed to all eligible employees and are also readily available upon request by employees.

Offering employee workshops and question and answer sessions can further increase plan participation. Employees who are not interested in reading the written materials might make time to attend a short workshop describing the plan. These workshops also give employees that do not understand the written materials a forum for asking questions. These workshops can be videotaped for employees that are unable to attend the scheduled workshops. A videotape of the workshops can also be easily distributed to remote company offices.

The following topics should be covered in the various employee communications:

- The company's objective(s) in establishing the plan.
- A description of the benefits of participating in the plan.
- Policies and procedures, including who to contact with questions about the plan.
- A description of the tax consequences to individual plan participants.

For publicly traded companies that have used Form S-8 to register the shares that will be issued pursuant to the ESPP, the written communications provided to employees should comply with the prospectus requirements specified in the instructions to Form S-8.

Providing a written plan summary and offering employee workshops is an excellent start, but it may be necessary to take additional steps to truly peak employee interest. Other ways you can publicize your ESPP include advertising the plan by displaying posters around the workplace, placing flyers advertising the plan in employee mailboxes, or including a brief notice on the stubs of employee paychecks. Distributing announcements using the company's electronic or voice mail system can also prove very effective and economically feasible. These additional marketing pieces do not have to describe the plan in full; instead, they are aimed at generating employee interest and encouraging employees to read the full written plan summary or attend one of the employee workshops.

Plan Enrollment

If the employee communication program is successful, employees will want to participate in the plan. Most plans have specified dates on which employees can enter the plan. Although there is no requirement that an ESPP operate this way, typically, after the initial entry date, a subsequent entry date will occur immediately following each purchase date. For example, if a plan has an initial entry date of January 1, with purchase dates occurring every 6 months thereafter, on June 30 and December 31, then typically, additional entry dates occur on each July 1 and January 1 following the purchase dates. On these additional entry dates, any employees who did not choose to participate originally or who became eligible to participate after the initial entry date are permitted to enter the plan. No employees are permitted to enter at any time other than the specified entry dates.

Distributing Enrollment Forms

Employees who want to participate in the plan are usually asked to complete an enrollment form before the entry date. The enrollment form typically requires the employee's name, address, Social Security number, date of enrollment, percentage of salary to be contributed to the plan, and the employee's signature. If employees are allowed to choose between several issuance methods, the enrollment form may also require the employee to indicate his or her preference on this matter. If the shares issued as a result of the employee purchases will not be registered in employee names, it may be necessary for employees to complete an additional form authorizing the company to issue the shares registered in the appropriate names.

Many companies reiterate some of the provisions of the plan in the enrollment form, including any limitations on participation, limitations on adjustments to contribution rates or withdrawals from the plan, determination of the purchase price, and any other provisions that are applicable to the employee's participation in the plan. The enrollment form may also include a statement that the purchase will occur automatically without further instruction from the employee, along with a statement that the employee has read and understood the plan or plan summary. By reiterating these provisions in the enrollment form, when the employee signs the enrollment form, the employee also agrees to all these terms and conditions of the plan. Where these plan provisions are not reiterated in the enrollment form, the company might have a separate form reiterating them, which the employee is also required to sign before enrolling in the plan.

Enrollment forms are usually distributed to employees a few weeks or a month before the enrollment deadline. The enrollment deadline might be the actual entry date, or it might be a few days before the entry date. Enrollment forms submitted after the enrollment deadline are generally not accepted. Reminder notices can be sent to employees a few days before this deadline to prevent an onslaught of submissions just one or two days after the deadline. These reminders can be sent via electronic or voice mail to have the maximum effect with minimal cost. Some companies print brief reminders on the stubs of employee paychecks.

Additional Communications

It may be necessary to redistribute the written plan materials and offer additional employee workshops before each entry date, especially for those employees who have been hired since the plan was initially implemented and therefore did not have an opportunity to receive this information at that time. To avoid redistributing this information to all employees, companies might instead include this information in new-hire orientations. Additional copies of the written plan materials can be available on request, or copies can be available in central locations around the workplace (perhaps on a company bulletin board). If the company has an intranet site, a relatively simple and effective way to make the plan summary and other documents available to employees, such as the list of frequently asked questions, is to post these documents on the site. If participation in the ESPP is discussed during new-hire orientations, it may not be necessary to hold ongoing employee workshops. A company might hold additional workshops once a year or might only hold additional workshops if plan participation levels seemed to be lagging.

Recordkeeping by the Stock Administrator

The stock administrator usually retains a record of all employee communications distributed before each entry date. This record serves as proof that employees were notified of their right to participate in the plan and of the plan procedures. This documentation could be important if an employee later challenges the company regarding some aspect of his or her participation in the plan.

Employees return their completed enrollment forms to the stock administrator, who typically makes a copy to be retained in the stock administration files and then forwards the originals to the payroll department. The payroll department arranges for the appropriate amounts to be withheld from employee paychecks and, since the enrollment form represents an authorization to have funds withheld from employee paychecks, typically retains the original enrollment form in its files.

It is generally not necessary for the stock administrator to record new enrollments at this time. If the stock administrator is using a spreadsheet to process the purchase, the spreadsheet will most likely be created just before the purchase date with the data the payroll department provides to the stock administrator regarding participant contributions. Where the stock administrator is using a database or a software program, employee enrollment data can be recorded at the time the enrollment form is received, but the stock administrator might want to consider the necessity of doing so. Not all employees that enroll in the plan ultimately participate in the purchase, some terminate their employment before the purchase date, and others may voluntarily withdraw from the plan before the purchase. By recording enrollment information when the enrollment form is received, the stock administrator may then have to delete this information before the purchase. Even if it is not necessary to delete this information, the stock administrator has spent time recording information that ultimately is not needed. Therefore, rather than recording enrollment information at the time enrollment forms are received, the stock administrator may simply forward the enrollment forms to the payroll department and record enrollment information just before the purchase date for only those individuals that actually participate in the purchase.

Contributions to the Plan

Since under most plans, contributions can be made only in the form of payroll deductions, the stock administrator relies on the payroll department to track contributions to the plan. The payroll department verifies the amounts contributed to the plan and that deductions are taken only from eligible compensation. If the plan permits contributions from base salary and commissions but does not permit contributions from bonuses or overtime pay, the payroll department must verify that the deductions are taken from salary and commissions only and that no deductions are taken from bonuses or overtime pay. Typically, the plan will limit the funds that can be contributed to a specified percentage of the employee's eligible compensation. The payroll department is responsible for verifying that this limit is not exceeded.

Changes in Plan Enrollment and Participation

From time to time, participants will terminate employment before the purchase date. The human resources department notifies the stock administrator and payroll department when a participant terminates. This notification can be provided to the stock administrator on a monthly, weekly, or participant-by-participant basis, as appropriate. Regardless of how often these notifications are provided, the stock administrator must be informed of any and all participant terminations before the purchase date. Typically, participants' rights to participate in the ESPP terminate with their termination of employment. Any contributions that have not been used to purchase shares are refunded without interest.

Occasionally, participants voluntarily terminate or withdraw their participation in the ESPP, even though they remain employed by the company. To withdraw from the plan, the participant is usually required to complete a form stating that he or she is withdrawing from the plan. This form, which may be the same form that is completed to enroll in the plan, typically indicates the date the withdrawal is effective and requires the participant's signature authorizing the withdrawal. The form typically states any limitations on the participant's ability to resume participation in the plan and clearly indicates if the withdrawal is effective immediately or upon the completion of the next purchase. Once the withdrawal form is completed, the participant's contributions to the plan cease and, if the withdrawal is effective immediately, any previous unused contributions are refunded. The stock administrator retains a copy of the withdrawal form, forwarding the original form to the payroll department so that payroll deductions can be stopped and any refunds can be processed.

Any amounts to be refunded can be included in the employee's next or final paycheck to minimize the administrative cost associated with processing refunds. Typically, the company does not pay interest on the amounts refunded to participants; therefore, these refunds should be completed with only a minimal delay.

Adjusting the Contribution Rate

Participants occasionally adjust their rate of contribution to the plan. To do so, the participant is usually required to complete a form authorizing the adjustment. This form, which may be the same form that is completed to enroll in the plan, indicates the date the adjustment is effective, the desired rate of contribution, and requires the participant's signature authorizing the adjustment. The form also typically states any limitations on the participant's ability to further adjust his or her contribution rate. The stock administrator retains a copy of the adjustment form, forwarding the original form to the payroll department, so that the participant's rate of contribution to the plan can be adjusted.

Preparing for the Purchase Date

The stock administrator will begin preparing for the purchase a week or two weeks before the purchase date. These preparations involve verifying and reconciling participant contributions and account information.

The payroll department notifies the stock administrator of the amounts each participant has contributed to the plan. This notification can be provided in a data file, so that the stock administrator does not have to manually record the contributed amounts in the spreadsheet, database, or software program that is used to calculate the shares each participant can purchase. Ideally, the payroll department provides the data in a format that can be directly imported into the stock administrator's system. If this is not possible, perhaps the payroll department can provide the data in a format that can be converted into a spreadsheet, which the stock administrator can then reformat and import.

The payroll department also generates and provides to the stock administrator a report listing each participant's contributions. If contributions have been imported into the stock administrator's system, this report is used to verify that the data transfer was successful. If the payroll department was not able to provide a data file, the stock administrator relies on this report to manually record the contributions. This report lists each participant's current contributions and also lists the prior balance in each participant's account. This allows the stock administrator to complete a more thorough verification of the data by comparing both the current contributions and the prior balances in his or her system to the report generated by the payroll department.

The contribution data and reports can be provided to the stock administrator after each payroll period ends, but it may be more efficient to provide all contribution data at once, along with one report, just before the purchase date. If the contribution data and reports are provided after each payroll period, the stock administrator must import or record this information each period and reconcile the data each period. When participants terminate their employment or withdraw from the plan before the purchase date, the stock administrator must delete the contribution data for those participants from the system. If the contribution data and report is sent once, just before the purchase date, the stock administrator imports or records that data just once and reconciles just once. The stock administrator does not have to delete current contributions for terminated or withdrawn employees because this information is not included in the data file (it may still be necessary to clear out prior balances, however).

Along with the contribution data and report, the payroll department also provides a list of participating employees. The stock administrator verifies that everyone on this list has contributed to the plan and that everyone who has contributed to the plan appears on this list. Any discrepancies are investigated and resolved before the purchase date.

The payroll department should provide the final contribution data and reports to the stock administrator as soon as this information is available, probably about a week before the purchase date. The stock administrator needs this time to verify the data and reconcile any discrepancies. All reconciling should be completed before the purchase date, so that the purchase can occur smoothly and efficiently.

It may also be necessary to verify each participant's issuance instructions. This can be accomplished by distributing a notice to each participant reviewing the issuance instructions provided by that participant. If the shares will be automatically sold or deposited in the participant's brokerage account, the notice may also include the name of the participant's brokerage firm and his or her account number at that firm. If a certificate registered in the participant's name will be issued, it may be necessary to verify the participant's address so that the certificate is not sent to an outdated address. As an alternative to distributing a customized notice to each participant, the stock administrator may simply distribute a general reminder that shares will be issued according to the instructions indicated in participant records and describe how participants can modify their issuance instructions. To minimize the cost and effort involved in distributing these notices, it is probably most effective to distribute them via electronic mail. If a participant's issuance instructions have not previously been obtained, it is necessary to obtain these instructions before the purchase date. Without this information, the issuance of the participant's shares could be delayed or misdirected.

The Purchase

The number of shares each participant can purchase is calculated by dividing the participant's purchase price into his or her total contributions. The plan document specifies how the purchase price is determined. The most common method of determining the price is to compare the fair market value on the date the participant entered the plan to the fair market value on the purchase date. The participant's purchase price is 85% of the lower of these two values. This is the minimum price required if the plan is to qualify for preferential tax treatment available under Section 423. This method can result in different prices for participants that entered the plan on different dates.

Plan Entry Dates and Purchase Dates

When a participant remains enrolled in the plan for multiple purchases, eventually it is necessary to update the entry date that is used for comparison purposes when determining the participant's purchase price. The frequency with which this date must be updated is specified in the plan and is commonly referred to as the offering period. In a plan with a 24-month offering period, the entry date for each participant must be updated at least every 24 months. Purchase dates may occur at more frequent intervals during this time period. For example, a plan may specify a 24-month offering period with purchase dates occurring at 6-month intervals. If an employee enters the plan on January 1, 1999, the employee's purchase price for the next four purchases is determined by comparing the fair market value on each purchase date to the fair market value on the employee's entry date, January 1, 1999. After the fourth purchase, on December 31, 2000, the employee has reached the end of the offering period and a new offering begins. The employee's entry date in the new offering is January 1, 2001. For the next four purchases (starting with the purchase on June 30, 2001), the employee's purchase price is determined by comparing the fair market value on the purchase date to the fair market value on January 1, 2001. After the last of these four purchases, a new offering period begins again and the employee's entry date is again reset. The employee's participation continues uninterrupted throughout this process. It is not necessary for the employee to complete any additional forms or sign any additional authorizations.

There is no requirement that the offering period be 24 months long. Frequently, plans specify offering periods that are 3, 6, or 12 months in length. There is also no requirement that purchase dates occur more than once during an offering. However, if the plan is intended to qualify for preferential tax treatment, the offering period defined in the plan must comply with the requirements of Section 423.

Determining Fair Market Value

The fair market value of a company's stock is usually the closing or average trading price of the day. Because the fair market value on the purchase date is often important in determining the purchase price, it may not be possible to determine the purchase price, or to calculate the number of shares each participant can purchase, before the market closes on the date of the purchase. For the purchase price to be correct, it must be based on accurate fair market values. The stock administrator should verify the fair market value on each participant's entry date and the purchase date before establishing the purchase price. It may be advisable to verify the trading prices with more than one source, especially if the stock administrator is relying on trading prices reported over the Internet.

Calculating the Number of Shares Purchased

After the purchase price has been determined, the stock administrator calculates the number of shares each participant can purchase. The stock administrator must verify that the number of shares purchased by each participant does not exceed any limits defined within the plan. If the plan is intended to qualify for preferential tax treatment, it is also necessary to verify that the number of shares purchased does not exceed the limit imposed by Section 423. This limit is $25,000 worth of stock per year, based on the fair market value on the date the participant entered the plan. If the number of shares any participant can purchase with his or her contributions exceeds either a limit defined within the plan or the limit imposed by Section 423, the participant is permitted to purchase only those shares that are within the limit. As a result, a portion of the funds contributed by the participant are not used to purchase shares. When a limit is exceeded, most plans provide that the funds that have not been used to purchases shares will be refunded to the participant without interest. The participant may want to reduce his or her rate of contribution, so as not exceed the limit for future purchases.

The stock administrator should also verify that the total number of shares purchased by all participants combined does not exceed the number of shares available for issuance under the plan. At the time of adoption, a specified number of shares are reserved and approved for issuance pursuant to the ESPP. A number of these shares are issued during each purchase, reducing the number of shares available for future purchases. If the total number of shares to be purchased by all participants combined exceeds the number of shares currently available for issuance under the plan, each participant's purchase will be prorated accordingly. For example, if the total number of shares that all participants combined can purchase is 10,000 shares but there are only 8,000 shares available for issuance under the plan, each participant purchases only 80% of the number of shares he or she could have purchased if all 10,000 shares had been available for issuance under the plan. This again results in a portion of each participant's contributions not being used to purchase shares. In this instance, most plans provide that the contributions that have not been used to purchase shares will be refunded to participants without interest.

Whole Shares vs. Fractional Shares

Generally, participants are permitted to purchase only whole shares. Rarely, if ever, will the amount each participant contributed to the plan be evenly divisible by the participant's purchase price. Dividing the purchase price into the participant's contributions almost always results in a fractional number of shares. Since the participant has not contributed enough to purchase any more than this amount, the fractional number is rounded down to the nearest whole share. As a result, every participant in the plan probably has a small amount of contributed funds (less than the price of one share) that have not been used to purchase shares. It could be administratively expensive for the company to refund these unused funds; therefore, most plans provide that these funds remain in participant accounts and are applied to the next purchase.

Communicating the Purchase Results

After determining the number of shares each participant can purchase, the stock administrator instructs the company's transfer agent to issue certificates for the shares that have been purchased. For participants who want to hold the shares in their name, a certificate is registered in the name of the participant and delivered to the participant. For participants who want to automatically sell or to have their shares deposited into brokerage accounts, the shares are registered in the name of the brokerage firm and delivered to the brokerage firm. These issuances can be completed electronically by Deposit/ Withdrawal at Custodian (DWAC), decreasing the time and expense associated with issuing shares. If participants are required to use a designated brokerage firm for automatic sales or deposits into brokerage accounts, one issuance is completed for all the shares registered to the brokerage firm. Since share issuances are charged to the company on a per-issuance basis, this can decrease the cost associated with issuing shares. Because of the expense involved, some companies have begun refusing to issue shares in employee names, requiring instead that employees establish an account with the company's designated brokerage firm and arrange for their shares to be deposited into this account.

Working with Your Transfer Agent and Brokerage Firm

The instructions provided to the transfer agent include the number of certificates to be issued, the number of shares to be issued in each certificate, the correct name under which the shares are to be registered, appropriate delivery instructions, and any restrictive legends which must be placed on the certificates. These instructions usually require the signature of an authorized company representative and are usually accompanied by a letter summarizing the total number of shares to be issued, the total number of certificates to be issued, the name of the plan under which the shares are to be issued, and the date of purchase. For any certificates that will be registered in employee names, the transfer agent can be instructed to note in their records that the certificate was issued pursuant to the ESPP. This notation appears in the transfer agent's records and in reports the transfer agent provides to the stock administrator; it does not appear on the certificate itself. This notation can be utilized later to assist in tracking dispositions of the stock. If only a small number of certificates are issued, as when the company has a designated brokerage firm, it may be sufficient to transmit a report to the transfer agent via fax. If a larger number of certificates are issued, as when the company does not have a designated brokerage firm, it may be advisable to transmit the issuance instructions in an electronic format, such as a spreadsheet file or other type of data file.

The stock administrator also provides a report to the company's designated brokerage firm, notifying the brokerage firm that it will be receiving the shares purchased pursuant to the ESPP. The brokerage firm receives one large certificate for all the shares registered to it. The report provided by the stock administrator instructs the brokerage firm on how many of these shares to deposit in each individual participant's account and how many shares to sell for each participant who has requested an automatic sale. It may be advisable to call the brokerage firm before sending the report, so that the brokerage firm expects a large number of shares and knows that a report is forthcoming describing how these shares are allocated among employee accounts.

The instructions provided to the brokerage firm include the name of each participant, the number of shares purchased by each participant, whether the shares are to be sold or deposited in participant accounts, and participant account numbers at the firm. The instructions also indicate whether the shares will be issued electronically via DWAC or whether actual certificates will be delivered to the brokerage firm. For cost and efficiency, electronic issuances are preferable to issuing actual certificates.

The transfer agent and designated brokerage firm are unable to proceed without instructions from the stock administrator. It is therefore necessary to provide these instructions with as minimal delay as possible. Where participants want to automatically sell their shares, the shares must be delivered to the brokerage firm quickly so that the sale can be completed. Delays could prevent participants from receiving the sale price they anticipate. Even when shares are not being sold, participants are eager to know how many shares they have purchased and to receive those shares or verify the share deposit in their brokerage account. After the purchase date arrives, only a day or two at most should elapse before the shares are automatically sold or deposited in the participants' brokerage accounts.

Discuss the arrangements for issuing shares with the company's transfer agent and designated brokerage firm well in advance of the first purchase. Specific transfer agents and brokers may have their own requirements and capabilities. It is important to know what information is required and the format it will be distributed in ahead of time so that shares can be issued without incident or delay once the purchase date arrives.

Communications to Participants

It is likely that the plan participants will be eager to learn the number of shares they purchased. The stock administrator might want to distribute a communication to the participants summarizing their purchases as soon as possible after the purchase date. Ideally, this communication is distributed within a few days to a week following the purchase date. If participants do not receive this communication, they may call the administrator inquiring about their purchase. The sooner this communication is distributed, the fewer of these inquiries the stock administrator will have to answer. To forestall participant inquiries, the stock administrator may want to make an announcement shortly after the purchase, perhaps even the next day, assuring participants that the purchase occurred, describing the purchase price (or, if there were multiple prices, how to determine the purchase price), explaining that participants can determine the number of shares they purchased by dividing the purchase price into their total contributions to the plan listed on their last paycheck, and confirming that participants will receive a statement of the number of shares they purchased within a specified time frame. This announcement may be distributed via electronic or voice mail or may be posted on the company's intranet site if such a site exists.

The statement provided to participants might include a summary of the offering period, the purchase date, the purchase price and how it was determined, the amount contributed to the plan, the number of shares purchased, how the shares are to be issued, and when the participant can expect to receive the shares or sale proceeds. If the participant can expect a refund, the statement might state the amount to be refunded to the participant and explain the reason for the refund. Participants should be instructed to retain the statement for tax purposes; if they have received shares (either in their name or in their brokerage accounts), they also should be instructed to notify the stock administrator when they sell these shares.

Payroll Department Responsibilities

The payroll department must reset participant accounts after the purchase occurs, clearing out the existing contributions in their records. The stock administrator informs the payroll department of any remaining balances in participant accounts and any amounts that must be refunded to participants. A file containing this data can be provided along with a report, so that the payroll department can import the remaining balances and/or refunds after clearing out all previous contributions. The payroll department should be able to identify these remaining balances in each participant's account so that it is possible to separate these amounts from future contributions. The payroll department issues refunds where necessary. Any amounts to be refunded can be included in the participant's next paycheck to minimize the cost to the company. Typically the company does not pay interest on the amounts refunded to participants; therefore, any refunds should be completed with as little delay as possible.

Reports to Management

The stock administrator might want to provide a report of the purchase to management. This report might include the number of employees who participated in the purchase, a comparison of the participation level for this purchase to previous purchases, the number of shares that were purchased, the number of participants that engaged in an automatic sale and the number of participants that did not, the purchase price, the fair market value on the purchase date, the participants' gain per share, and the number of remaining shares available for issuance under the plan.

Special Procedures for Company Officers

In addition to the above-mentioned procedures, officers of the company that participate in the plan may require special reporting and administrative procedures. Officers, because of their role in the company, are subject to laws and regulations that do not apply to other employees. Care must be taken to ensure that their participation in the ESPP complies with these regulations. In particular, it is desirable to ensure that purchases made by officers under the plan are exempt from the operation of Section 16(b) of the Securities Exchange Act of 1934. Shares purchased through an ESPP must be included in the number of shares beneficially owned by the officer when filing the reports required for officers under Section 16(a). If the purchase is not exempt from the operation of Section 16(b), the purchase itself must also be included on these reports. Most officers are considered affiliates of the company, and as such, they generally must comply with the requirements of Rule 144 of the Securities Act of 1933 when selling company stock. For affiliates that engage in an automatic sale, the sale must comply with Rule 144. The stock administrator may be responsible for ensuring that these requirements are met or may act in partnership with the legal department or corporate secretary to ensure this compliance.

Financial Reporting for the Plan

A purchase of shares pursuant to the ESPP is reflected in the company's financial statements. The stock administrator provides a report of each purchase to the accounting or finance department so that the purchase can be properly accounted for in the shareholders' equity section of the company's balance sheet. This report includes the total number of shares purchased and the total purchase price. An audit of the purchase listing the number of shares purchased and the price paid by each individual participant may also be required. This information is provided to the accounting or finance department before the next series of financial statements must be prepared for the company.

It is possible that an employee stock purchase will, in some situations, result in an expense to the company. In some cases, this expense is recognized in the company's income statement; in other situations, this expense can be disclosed in a footnote to the company's financial statements. The accounting or finance department should carefully review the accounting treatment applicable to the company's ESPP to determine whether these potential expenses apply to the company's plan.

Dispositions of Shares Acquired Pursuant to the Plan

The company has a reporting obligation for tax purposes when participants dispose of shares acquired pursuant to an ESPP that qualifies for preferential tax treatment under Section 423. Upon disposition of shares acquired through a Section 423 plan, the employee recognizes compensation income. The company must furnish an employee who disposes of shares acquired through a Section 423 plan with a Form W-2 for the year of the disposition reporting the compensation income recognized as "wages." Additionally, if the disposition does not qualify for preferential tax treatment (a "disqualifying disposition"), the company is entitled to a tax deduction equal to the amount of compensation reported on the employee's Form W-2.

Under Code Section 6039, the company has an obligation to provide in writing certain basic information about the shares acquired under a Section 423 plan to each participant in connection with the first transfer of legal title of such shares in a disposition that qualifies for preferential tax treatment (a "qualifying disposition").

Recording Disqualifying Dispositions Resulting from Automatic Sales

To fulfill its reporting obligations and receive its tax deduction, the company must first learn that the employee has disposed of shares acquired through the plan. An automatic sale of shares following the purchase will always be a disqualifying disposition. The stock administrator automatically records these shares as disposed and also records the compensation income recognized by each participant and the corresponding tax deduction for the company. The software program or spreadsheet in which the dispositions are recorded is usually designed to calculate the participant's compensation income and company tax deduction for the stock administrator.

Tracking Dispositions of Shares Deposited in Brokerage Accounts or Issued in Employee Names

Shares deposited in a brokerage account are beneficially owned by the account holder. The stock administrator periodically sends a letter or survey to the account holder, inquiring if these shares have been sold or otherwise disposed. If shares are held in accounts at the company's designated brokerage firm, the firm may be able to inform the stock administrator when the shares are sold or otherwise transferred from these accounts. Ideally, the brokerage firm transmits this information to the stock administrator in a data file that can be uploaded into the stock administrator's spreadsheet or software program. If not, the stock administrator must manually record these dispositions. Once the dispositions have been recorded, the spreadsheet or software program calculates and records the employee's compensation income and company tax deduction associated with each disposition.

The company's transfer agent may be able to assist in tracking dispositions of shares that have been issued in employee names. To sell or dispose of these shares, employees must transfer the title of the shares. If, when the shares were originally issued, the transfer agent noted that the certificate was issued pursuant to the ESPP, the transfer agent should be able to notify to the stock administrator when the employees transfer the titles of these shares. Unfortunately, it is unlikely that the transfer agent will know the nature of the transfers. Not all transfers are considered dispositions. Upon receiving a notice from the transfer agent that a certificate has been transferred, the stock administrator sends a letter or survey to the employee that held the certificate, inquiring about the nature of the transfer.

The letter or survey includes a brief explanation of reason for the inquiry, the number shares which are no longer held in the employee's name, the date the shares in question were acquired by the employee, the date the title of the shares was transferred, and the purchase price of the shares. The survey asks the employee to confirm the transfer date and the current status of the shares (sold, gifted, held in the employee's brokerage account, etc.). If the shares have been sold, the survey also requests the sale price. Most Section 423 plans require participants to notify the company upon disposition of shares acquired pursuant to the plan. It may be helpful to explain this requirement in the survey. It also may be beneficial to explain that completing the survey does not in any way change the employee's tax obligation, but it does fulfill the employee's obligation to notify the company of the disposition. The survey is retained in the stock administrator's files at least until the completed survey has been returned. Surveys can be distributed three or four times per year so that the stock administrator is only recording three or four months of transfers at a time. If surveys are not distributed until the end of the year, the stock administrator is forced to record a full year of transfers at a time that is already very busy.

The stock administrator records the disposition when surveys are returned indicating that the shares have been sold or otherwise disposed. Once the dispositions have been recorded, the software program calculates and records the employee's compensation income and company tax deduction associated with each disposition. The completed survey is retained in the stock administrator's files.

Employees do not always return the surveys the first time they are distributed. The stock administrator may have to distribute follow-up letters and may even follow up with phone calls. Because the company has a reporting obligation, and because the tax deduction for disqualifying dispositions can be substantial, dispositions should not be neglected. But in some cases, the administrative effort and cost involved in researching dispositions may outweigh the penalties for not doing so. The stock administrator should consult the company's tax advisors to determine how much effort should be extended to pursue dispositions.

Requiring employees to use a designated brokerage firm can greatly facilitate tracking dispositions. If shares are issued in employee names, or if employees are permitted to use any brokerage firm, the stock administrator must rely on employees to find out when the shares have been disposed. But, if the employees that engage in an automatic sale are required to use a designated brokerage firm, the stock administrator knows, without any research, that the shares have been sold. If employees that do not want to sell are required to arrange for their shares to be deposited and held in accounts at the company's designated brokerage firm, the brokerage firm can notify the stock administrator when shares are sold or transferred out of these accounts. This could largely eliminate the necessity of surveying employees regarding their dispositions.

Information Provided to the Payroll Department

A listing of dispositions is provided to the payroll department on a quarterly basis so that the payroll department can update the compensation income recorded for each employee in their records. For disqualifying dispositions, the report typically includes the name of the employee, the number of shares disposed, the employee's entry date and purchase date, the purchase price of the shares, the fair market value on the purchase date, the compensation income to be recognized by the employee, and the company tax deduction for each transaction. The company must fulfill its Form W-2 reporting obligation with regard to the compensation income recognized by the employee to be eligible for the tax deduction. For qualifying dispositions, the report includes the name of the employee, the number of shares disposed, the employee's entry date and purchase date, the fair market value on the employee's entry date and purchase date, the purchase price, the sale price, and the compensation income to be recognized by the employee. The company is not entitled to a tax deduction for qualifying dispositions.

Information Provided to Employees

For qualifying dispositions, the stock administrator also provides a statement to the employee containing certain basic information about the disposed shares. The statement, required under Code Section 6039, includes the name and address of the company, the name, address and social security number of the employee transferring the shares, the date the shares were transferred to the employee, the number of shares transferred, and the type of option under which the shares were acquired. This statement must be provided to the employee no later than the January 31 following the year in which the shares were first transferred.

Conclusion

The process of administering an ESPP, from plan design to purchase to disposition, can seem overwhelming. Each component must be broken down and completed one step at a time, but with a view to the next step. First design the plan, then develop policies and procedures. Design the forms that will be used for enrollment, adjustments and withdrawals. Establish channels of communication between the payroll department, the stock administrator, and the human resources department. Establish communications with the company's transfer agent and designated brokerage firm. Develop a program for announcing the plan to employees and for ongoing employee communications. Establish procedures to fulfill tax and accounting reporting obligations.

Once these procedures are in place, the plan usually operates smoothly and efficiently. Procedures may be revised slightly as time passes, but it is not necessary to rewrite them for every purchase. Creating these procedures can require a substantial initial investment but can also result in a plan that is highly valued and respected by both employees and the company.

Author's Note: I would like to thank Fran Brooks for her assistance with this chapter. As an experienced stock plan administrator, Fran offered me her insights into the mechanics of administering an ESPP and answered many questions for me. Her expertise was very valuable to my research for this chapter.

CHAPTER 3

Accounting for Employee Stock Purchase Plans

Donna Lowe

Employee stock purchase plans (ESPPs) help employees buy employer stock on favorable terms. In the relatively stable markets of days gone by, these plans provided an efficient way to purchase stock with relatively small transaction fees, if any. In those days the primary purposes of maintaining an ESPP was not to compensate employees but rather to aid them with purchases of employer stock. However, in a strong economy with a volatile stock market, the compensation element provided by ESPPs can be substantial.

Under Section 423 of the Internal Revenue Code (the "Code"), ESPPs may qualify for special tax treatment if they satisfy certain criteria. Many plans maximize the benefit afforded employees under the Code by using a look-back provision. This allows employees to contribute to the plan during an offering period and then purchase the employer's stock for at a discount of up to 15% from either the fair market value at the beginning of the offering period or the end of the period, whichever is lower.

While many ESPPs are designed to meet the requirements of Section 423, there is an increasing number of newly designed plans that do not meet these criteria. Many companies are finding that the criteria of Section 423 do not coincide with the company's strategic purpose or other objections of an employee stock purchase plan. Like all compensation and benefit programs, the primary focus for the plan design should be the company's business mission and objectives. The first question asked when determining if an employee stock purchase plan is appropriate should be, "How would it fit into our total compensation and benefits package to support the company's business mission?"

The remainder of this chapter will discuss the accounting issues associated with ESPPs. This chapter will not distinguish between plans that satisfy the criteria of Section 423 of the Code from those that are not "qualified," because this distinction is not critical to the determination of the accounting treatment of such plans. Furthermore, it is also important to note that recording a compensation expense on the financial statements does not coincide with taking a tax deduction. Since accounting rules and tax rules are created by different groups with different purposes, they are not interdependent and seldom correlate.

The accounting rules are especially important to publicly held companies because financial measurements taken from the financial statements filed with the SEC are commonly used by investors to measure the financial health of the company. Thus, when a stock-based compensation plan can avoid an accounting charge altogether, it is likely a substantial benefit to the company.

Privately held companies typically do not have ESPPs because there are significant securities issues associated with selling stock to the broad employee group. Recently, however, a growing number of privately held companies have started using ESPPs in spite of the hurdles presented by the securities laws. Privately held companies that move in this direction need to be cautious about recognizing a compensation expense associated with the plan because it may affect their ability to get loans, the cost of loans, or their ability to abide by loan covenants or similar documents. Additionally, companies that hope to go public should consider how the accounting considerations associated with ESPPs might affect the feasibility of an initial public offering.

Under the current accounting rules for equity-based compensation arrangements, there are two categories of plans that do not result in a compensation expense. Plans in the first category are those defined as noncompensatory. Plans in the second category are those that are considered compensatory in which the amount of the compensation expense happens to equal zero. Before plunging into the current rules, which are somewhat less than intuitive, it is helpful to consider the origin of the rules.

The History of Accounting for Equity-Based Compensation

As background for the rules discussed in the rest of this chapter, this section provides a brief history of the evolution of the accounting rules associated with equity-based compensation.

Early Standards

In November 1948, the Committee on Accounting Procedure of the American Institute of Certified Public Accountants (AICPA) released the first guidelines for accounting for compensatory stock options, Accounting Research Bulletin No. 37. After favorable tax treatment was introduced to the Code in 1950 for certain qualified stock options, the popularity of equity-based compensation grew quickly. In 1953, the AICPA released Accounting Research Bulletin No. 43. Although these early versions of qualified stock options are very different from what we commonly use today, they provided the impetus and framework for the plans we now have.

1972: The AICPA Issues APB 25

In 1972, the AICPA's Accounting Principles Board issued the first detailed set of accounting rules for equity-based compensation, "Accounting Principles Board Opinion 25: Accounting for Stock Issued to Employees" ("APB 25"). It became effective for all awards granted after December 31, 1972. Under this pronouncement, most ESPPs were considered noncompensatory and, as such, did not result in a compensation expense. For several years following the release of this pronouncement, many experts in the area felt that the economic substance of stock options and related plans was not appropriately considered. In addition to this shortfall, there were several questions left unanswered by this pronouncement, including a precise definition of its scope.

1993: The FASB Issues SFAS 123

In light of these concerns, in 1993, the Financial Accounting Standards Board (FASB), which in 1973 assumed responsibility for establishing accounting standards, proposed a pronouncement that would require employers to recognize the "fair value" of equity-based compensation on the face of the financial statements. Due to great opposition, this proposal was revised to encourage expense recognition on the face of the financial statements, but offer an alternative footnote disclosure for awards covered by APB 25. This footnote must disclose the pro forma effect of recognition of the fair value on net income and earnings per share. This pronouncement, "Statement of Financial Accounting Standards No. 123 Accounting for Stock-Based Compensation" ("SFAS 123"), was released in October 1995 and is effective for all awards granted during fiscal years beginning after December 15, 1994.

It is important to note that under the final version of SFAS 123, companies elect whether or not to adopt the recognition provisions. If a company elects to adopt the recognition provisions of SFAS 123, the election cannot be reversed. Consequently, the company is required to book an earnings charge for the fair value of stock-based compensation for all future periods. However, if a company does not elect to implement the recognition provisions of SFAS 123, the company must provide a footnote disclosure of the pro forma effect of applying the recognition provisions.

Whether the value of options is recognized or disclosed in the footnotes to the financial statements, the value associated with the stock options is the "fair value" of the options. SFAS 123 defines the fair value of options as the amount determined by a model that considers six basic factors: (1) the fair market value of the underlying stock; (2) the exercise price of the option; (3) the volatility of the underlying stock; (4) the expected term of the option; (5) the expected dividend yield of the underlying stock; and (6) the risk-free interest rate.

When this model is applied to ESPPs, the value associated with the plan is determined based on the substantive components of the plan. Thus, if the plan is designed to provide the equivalent of 85% of an option and 15% of a share of stock, the value associated with a participant's opportunity to purchase a single share is 85% of the option value plus 15% of the fair value of a share of stock. The final section of this chapter further elaborates on the substantive components and calculation of the compensation expense.

2000: The FASB Issues Interpretation No. 44

Since the original intent of SFAS 123 was to supersede APB 25, there was no attempt to provide further clarification for the many unanswered questions left by APB 25. However, when it became clear that most companies were choosing not to implement the recognition provisions of SFAS 123, generally relegating it to the level of footnote disclosure, the FASB began working to "clean up" APB 25, since this is what most companies were still using to determine a compensation expense. The final pronouncement from this "clean up" is titled FASB Interpretation No. 44 and became available on March 31, 2000. The provisions of Interpretation 44 that apply to ESPPs are effective July 1, 2000.

Since most companies did not adopt the recognition provisions of SFAS 123, the rules of APB 25 and Interpretation 44 usually determine the amount and timing of any accounting expense associated with stock-based compensation, including ESPPs.

This is very important to ESPPs, because many ESPPs are noncompensatory under the provisions of APB 25 and Interpretation 44 but are compensatory under SFAS 123.

Therefore, although companies will not recognize a compensation expense on their financial statements associated with an ESPP, they will still have to calculate the fair value of providing participants with an opportunity to purchase shares and disclose this expense in a footnote. The required footnote requires detailed calculations and is relatively lengthy.

The 4-Step Process for All ESPPs

With the history of the accounting rules as background, we need to understand how to analyze ESPPs under the current rules. Proper accounting for an ESPP, as for stock options or other stock-based compensation, is a four-step process:

1. The first step is to determine which accounting pronouncement is appropriate. It is possible for an ESPP to cover individuals who are employees under the definition provided in the Code but who are not employees under the definition provided in Interpretation 44. In this case, only those awards granted to "employees," as defined in Interpretation 44, will be under APB 25. Other awards will be considered nonemployee awards and will be subject to SFAS 123 (and Technical Bulletin 97-1).

2. The second step is to determine whether the plan is compensatory or noncompensatory under the relevant accounting pronouncement. If the plan is noncompensatory, there will not be an accounting expense associated with it. For companies who have not adopted the recognition provisions of SFAS 123, APB 25 and Interpretation 44 apply. For all nonemployee awards and all companies who have adopted the recognition provisions of SFAS 123, SFAS 123 applies. These standards differ significantly.

3. If a plan is compensatory, the third step is to determine the amount and timing of the accounting charge. If there is an accounting charge, it must be booked. Remember, a compensatory plan may have an accounting charge equal to zero. For most companies, this is determined under the rules of APB 25 and Interpretation 44.

4. Regardless of whether the plan is compensatory or not, the final step is to make the appropriate disclosures regarding the plan. SFAS 123 governs footnote disclosures and requires general disclosures about the plan regardless of materiality.

APB 25 and Interpretation 44

Since most ESPPs are noncompensatory under APB 25 and Interpretation 44, applying the accounting rules is relatively easy, because only the footnote disclosure is required. However, if there are features in an ESPP that make it compensatory under APB 25 and Interpretation 44, an accounting charge may be required. In all cases, appropriate footnote disclosure is required.

Compensatory vs. Noncompensatory

APB 25 uses language that generally covers both traditional stock options as well as ESPPs. Since an employee receives the right to purchase stock at the time the employee elects to contribute money to an ESPP, the substance of the plan is to grant the employee an option to purchase the shares.

Under APB 25, most ESPPs have been considered noncompensatory. The original language of APB 25 says:

> The Board concludes that at least four characteristics are essential in a noncompensatory plan:
> (a) substantially all full-time employees meeting limited employment qualifications may participate (employees owning a specified percent of the outstanding stock and executives may be excluded),
> (b) stock is offered to eligible employees equally or based on a uniform percentage of salary or wages (the plan may limit the number of shares of stock that an employee may purchase through the plan),
> (c) the time permitted for exercise of an option or purchase right is limited to a reasonable period, and
> (d) the discount from the market price of the stock is no greater than would be reasonable in an offer of stock to stockholders or others. An example of a noncompensatory plan is the "statutory" ESPP that qualifies under section 423 of the Internal Revenue Code.[1]

During late 1987 and early 1988, EITF 87-23: "Book Value Stock Purchase Plans" provided additional guidance on ESPPs. This pronouncement applies to companies that determine the value of the stock purchased using a formula (e.g., book value). Privately held companies typically do this to avoid having to do regular valuations. This pronouncement is of particular interest for privately held companies, because they are more likely to have book value plans.

Under this guidance, employers with book value stock purchase plans recognize no compensation expense if the employee "makes a substantive investment that will be at risk for a reasonable period of time." Since most ESPPs require the employees to pay 85% of the fair market value of the stock, employees are considered to make the substantive investment. So, plans that are designed to encourage ownership, i.e., the employer does not repurchase the shares quickly, will not give rise to an accounting charge.

In the years following the release of SFAS 123, FASB looked at the standards of APB 25. During the discussions leading up to Interpretation 44, the issue of a look-back provision was carefully scrutinized. Code Section 423 allows plans to use a look-back provision that allows employees to get a discount from the lower of the fair market value at the beginning of the offering period and the fair market value at the end of the offering period.

In the final version of Interpretation 44, FASB declared that a look-back provision will not cause an otherwise non-compensatory plan to be compensatory.

Amount and Timing of the Charge to Earnings

If an ESPP is compensatory because it does not meet the requirements outlined above, the amount and timing of an accounting charge will be determined based on the usual rules under APB 25 and Interpretation 44. For example, plans that offer more than a 15% discount will be considered compensatory.

If the plan is compensatory, then the accounting charge is determined based on whether the option is subject to fixed or variable accounting. In order to use fixed accounting, both the number of shares and the price of the shares must be known at the beginning of the offering period. Thus, if the number of shares purchased by each employee and the price at which the shares will be purchased is known at the beginning of the offering period, the charge is fixed at that time and is equal to the difference between the then-current fair market value of the share of stock and the purchase price. However, if either the number of shares or the price is not known at the beginning of the offering period, this will trigger variable accounting treatment, and the accounting charge will be variable until the offering period closes. Therefore, during the offering period the difference between the fair market value of the stock and the purchase price of the shares will be taken as a charge to earnings each accounting period until the end of the offering period.

For example, say that a company with a December 31 year-end has an ESPP with six-month offering periods that begin each April 1 and October 1. On December 31, the company will have an accounting charge that equals the sum of the accounting charge associated with the offering periods that closed on March 31 and September 30 during the year as well as an additional charge for the intrinsic value of the options that are outstanding for the offering period that began on October 1.

Shareholder Approval

If a plan is subject to shareholder approval, a measurement date under APB 25 cannot occur before the date such shareholder approval is obtained. This is especially important for 423 plans, because the Code requires shareholder approval, but allows it to be obtained within 12 months before or after of the effective date of the plan. For all practical purposes, most sponsors of 423 plans will want to obtain shareholder approval before the effective date of any awards under the plan. If management and the members of the board of directors have sufficient voting power to approve the plan, shareholder approval is deemed a formality and will not delay the measurement date for accounting purposes.

SFAS 123

Because most companies do not elect the recognition provisions of SFAS 123, its application is limited to a footnote disclosure (except as noted above). However, since SFAS 123 requires pro forma disclosure of the pro forma effect, the same determinations and calculations must be made. It is important to note that this is a complex calculation. This calculation is based on using an option pricing model such as Black-Scholes, which is most common. The following discussion describes the determinations and calculations required for the SFAS 123 footnote.

Compensatory vs. Noncompensatory

SFAS 123 provides the following criteria for ESPPs to be considered noncompensatory:

a.   The plan incorporates no option features other than the following, which may be incorporated:

   (1)   Employees are permitted a short period of time— not exceeding 31 days—after the purchase price has been fixed to enroll in the plan.

   (2)   The purchase price is based solely on the stock's market price at the date of purchase, and employees are permitted to cancel participation before the purchase date and obtain a refund of amounts previously paid (such as those paid by payroll withholdings).

b.   The discount from the market price does not exceed the greater of (1) a per-share discount that would be reasonable in recurring offer of stock to stockholders or others or (2) the per-share amount of stock issuance costs avoided by not having to raise a significant amount of capital by a public offering. A discount of 5 percent or less from the market price shall be considered to comply with this criterion without further justification.

c.   Substantially all full-time employees that meet limited employment qualifications may participate on an equitable basis.[2]

SFAS 123 allows some ESPPs to be considered noncompensatory (not valued and included in a pro forma expense), but most ESPPs are compensatory under SFAS 123 and must be valued. However, plans that meet the requirements listed above are noncompensatory. If a plan is noncompensatory, any discount reduces the proceeds for issuing the shares, but does not appear elsewhere in the financial statements, i.e., as a compensation expense on the income statement.[3]

The illustrations and discussion that follow assume that the plan is compensatory. Under SFAS 123, the most common feature that causes ESPPs to be compensatory is a look-back feature. Since most companies design their ESPPs with a look-back feature, most plans will be compensatory under SFAS 123. A look-back feature allows the purchase price to be determined at either the beginning or end of the offering period.[4] A typical plan with a look-back option, six-month window period, and 15% discount would work as follows where the price falls between the beginning and end of the period (i.e., where the look-back feature comes into play):

Fair market value at the beginning of the period	$12.00
Fair market value at the end of the period	$10.00
Discount	15%
Employee purchase price	$8.50

. . . and as follows when the price rises between the beginning and end of the period:

Fair market value at the beginning of the period	$9.00
Fair market value at the end of the period	$10.00
Discount	15%
Employee purchase price	$7.65

Valuation of Compensatory ESPPs Under SFAS 123

Without a Look-back Provision The general rule where an employee purchases property (employer stock or other property) is that the compensation expense included in the income statement will be the difference between the fair market value of the property and the amount the employee pays for the property. If there is no discount, there will be no charge. The amount of the accounting charge is determined as of the date of the transaction. However, if an employer grants an option to purchase stock (or other property), the charge is determined as of the date of grant and the value of the option must be calculated using an option-pricing model.

With a Look-back Provision In 1995, SFAS 123 established a general framework for calculating the fair value of ESPPs with look-back features. In its 1997 Technical Bulletin 97-1 ("TB 97-1"), FASB expanded this framework to apply to more types of look-back features. The original framework described in SFAS 123 is included in TB 97-1 as the type A plan.

The intent of TB 97-1 is to ensure that the substance of a look-back provision is viewed as the sum of its parts. There are essentially three analyses involved: (1) Determine whether the number of shares is fixed at the beginning of the window period or at the end of the window period; (2) determine whether the window periods are single (stand alone) periods or multiple (linked) periods; and (3) determine whether the employee withholdings can be changed during the window period. These analyses and the calculations associated with each are described in table 3-1 below.

Pursuant to FASB Technical Bulletin No. 97-1, there are nine designated types of ESPPs containing look-back features, each with a different valuation methodology based on the combinations of features described in the three analyses above:

1. Type A Plans set the number of shares that may be purchased by each employee at the beginning of the window period. Thus, if the stock price declines, the employee will not be able to purchase more shares. Instead, the employee will have unused withholdings returned.

2. Type B Plans allow employees to purchase as many shares as their salary withholdings will purchase.

3. Type C Plans allow employees to purchase as many shares as their salary withholdings will purchase, but use multiple purchase dates. Thus, an employee who elects to participate on January 1, 1998, could purchase shares at 85% of the lower of the price on January 1, 1998, or June

30, 1998, with withholdings set aside between these dates. Then, on January 1, 1999, the employee could purchase stock at the lower of the fair market value on January 1, 1998, or January 1, 1999, with amounts withheld between June 30, 1998, and January 1, 1999.

4. Type D plans allow employees to purchase shares based on an initial election carried over multiple purchase periods. This arrangement allows the front-end price to be reset each time a withholding period ends with a lower price.

5. Type E plans allow employees to purchase shares based on an initial election carried over multiple purchase periods, but rolls the election period forward each time a withholding period ends with a lower price.

6. Type F plans allow withholding changes between multiple purchase periods.

7. Type G plans allow withholding changes during a single purchase period.

8. Type H plans allow withholding changes at any time during or between multiple purchase periods.

9. Type I plans allow retrospective withholding changes by allowing employees to pay cash into the plan.

Conclusion

As companies continue to use ESPPs to reward employees, it is important to keep in mind the accounting issues associated with these plans. Since most of these plans will not cause an accounting charge, many companies may overlook the fact that certain design features may cause a charge. Moreover, most companies need professional assistance to analyze the plan and calculate the values required for the SFAS 123 footnote. Until now, the accounting rules have presented uncertainty. After being clarified, however, they continue to present complexity.

Table 3-1. Technical Bulletin 97-1 Analysis

Step 1	Number of Shares	*Fixed at Beginning of the Window Period*	*Variable Until the End of the Window Period*
		Value of Award = % discount × FMV share + (1 - % discount) × Call Option	Value of Award = % discount × FMV share + % discount × Put Option + (1- % discount) × Call Option
Step 2	Purchase Periods	*Single Purchase Period*	*Multiple Purchase Periods*
		Awards are valued at the beginning of each purchase period, and expense is allocated only to the accounting periods that coincide with the purchase period.	Awards are valued aggregately for multiple purchase periods at the beginning of the first purchase period and allocated to all accounting periods before and coinciding with the period of actual purchase. For example, a two-year purchase period may consist of four linked multiple periods. Options for all four periods would be valued at the beginning of the first period and valued in four tranches with expected terms of .5, 1.0, 1.5, and 2 years. Triggering a reset or rollover mechanism is treated as a modification of the original award.
Step 3	Withholdings	*Fixed Withholdings*	*Variable Withholdings*
		If employees are not permitted to change withholding elections during the window period, no additional modifications to the valuation methodology are needed.	If employees are permitted to change withholding elections during the window period, changes are treated as modifications to the original awards. The value of the modification is determined when the change is made, and the resulting expense is allocated to accounting periods prospectively to all accounting periods before and coinciding with the actual purchase period.

Notes

1. APB 25 ¶7.
2. SFAS 123 ¶23.
3. Ibid.
4. SFAS 123 ¶24.

CHAPTER 4

Getting the Most Out of Your ESPP

Joseph Lazur, Paul Rangecroft, and Al Schlachtmeyer

Today, companies all over the world are placing new emphasis on selecting, developing and focusing their employees to support the goals of the business. Managing talent effectively has become a management mantra for the new century. From 360-degree feedback to paid time-off banks, HR professionals are applying a variety of innovative approaches to help their organizations become faster, smarter, and more effective. In many quarters, this trend has merged with the idea of aligning the wealth of the company to the wealth of the people who produce it.

Wealth alignment initiatives often center on employer equity. In fact, an unprecedented amount of total compensation is now being delivered to all levels of the workforce through some form of company stock. At the executive level, companies are using stock option mega-grants to attract and retain mission-critical employees. Incentive systems are being re-crafted to include employer stock or its surrogate. Stock option reloads and repricing are debated intensely in the human resources trade press.

Companies are using four major vehicles to bring equity ownership down to the shop floor: employee stock ownership plans (ESOPs), 401(k) plans, broad-based stock option plans, and employee stock purchase plans (ESPPs).

More and more companies are implementing ESPPs. This growth is evident when one compares the 1998 survey results of the National Association of Stock Plan Professionals (NASPP) with corresponding results from the 1996 NASPP survey. In 1998, almost 53% of responding companies reported having an ESPP, while only 39% reported one in 1996. Additionally, 1998–1999 Total Salary Increase Survey from the American Compensation Association (now WorldatWork) found that over half of 3,000 participating companies had some sort of stock purchase plan. Despite this growth, there remains a lack of knowledge about what makes for a successful plan and how to go about implementing one. Certainly, most would agree that one primary measure of success is the percentage of employees actually participating in the plan and purchasing stock. This article discusses how certain plan design features and communication strategies can lead to a higher percentage of employees purchasing stock through these plans.

The Basics of Stock Purchase Plans

Standard Design Features

A stock purchase plan is a benefit program that lets employees accumulate their own funds (typically on an after-tax payroll deduction basis) toward the purchase of company stock, often at a discount. The money builds up over a set period of time. Then, a licensed broker takes the money, combines it with any subsidy the employer provides, buys company shares on the open market, and deposits them in the employee's account. At that point, employees can sell and realize a gain, or hold onto the stock. We have seen gains of 30% or more realized by plan participants in actively traded high-tech companies.

At the most basic level, a plan can simply provide employees with a convenient payroll deduction facility. Beyond that, the employer can choose from a wide array of optional design features to make the program more appealing to employees or to satisfy certain tax qualification rules. For example, a sponsoring company can vary the level of employer subsidy, the date at which the purchase price is determined, the accumulation period for employee dollars, and the limit on the amount of stock an employee can purchase, to name just a few.

Employer Subsidy

The employer subsidy may either be provided through a *discount* in the purchase price or a company *match* on the top of the employee's contribution. (A match in an ESPP is very similar to a company match in a 401(k)—the employer credits a participant's account with a fixed percentage of the employee's own contribution, say fifteen cents on the dollar.) When a discount is used, it is common to see the stock price discounted by 15%. This provides an incentive that adds to the normal wealth-building opportunities associated with common stock investing.

Purchase Price Date

The choice of purchase price date is another feature that can greatly enhance the value of an ESPP program to the employee. Some plans set the purchase price equal to the stock's price at the date shares are purchased. Others fix the purchase price to the stock's price at the beginning of the accumulation period, much like the grant date price for a typical stock option program. In fact, many ESPPs are designed to provide the best of all possible worlds. They have a purchase price set to be the lesser of the market price at the start of the accumulation period, or the market price at the end of the accumulation period. This is commonly referred to as a "look-back feature" and can greatly increase the value of the benefit provided to the plan participant.

Table 4-1 shows just how valuable this feature can be, even in a period of *declining* stock prices. Let's take a company with stock trading at $100 per share. Assume the plan provides a 15% discount on the lesser of the beginning or end of period stock price, and an employee contributes $1,000 during the purchase period.

As table 4-1 shows, even if the stock price declines over the accumulation period, the employee can come out ahead.

Table 4-1. Illustration of Look-Back Feature

	Change in Stock Price		
	Decreasing	Flat	Increasing
1. Stock Price Change over Purchase Period	−10%	0%	+10%
2. Stock Price at Beginning of Period	$ 100	$ 100	$ 100
3. Stock Price at End of Period	$ 90	$ 100	$ 110
4. Purchase Price Before Discount	$ 90	$ 100	$ 100
5. Purchase Price with Discount [(4) × 85%]	$ 76.50	$ 85.00	$ 85.00
6. Number of Shares Purchased [$1,000 ÷ (5)]	13.07	11.76	11.76
7. End of Period Value [(3) × (6)]	$ 1,176	$ 1,176	$ 1,294
8. Gain on $1,000 Investment	$ 176	$ 176	$ 294
9. Rate of Return	17.6%	17.6%	29.4%

Accumulation Period

The accumulation period is simply the period of time over which employee contributions build up before shares are actually purchased. The employee's money is set aside each pay period, and it may or may not accumulate with interest. Accumulation periods can range from weekly to two years or more. In general, most plans set the period to be somewhere between one and twelve months.

Qualified vs. Nonqualified

For tax treatment purposes, an ESPP will fall into one of two groups: those that qualify for special tax treatment and those that do not. Most ESPPs are the former, qualified under IRS Code Section 423. These plans, commonly known as "423 plans," provide some tax advantages to employees that can translate into increased participation rates. This difference in the tax treatment of a qualified and nonqualified plan also plays a role in the decision process at some companies. A company offering a nonqualified plan receives a tax deduction on the entire subsidy provided to employees when the shares are purchased, i.e., the difference between the discounted price and the fair market value when the stock is purchased. Of course, the employee loses potential tax benefits in this design, and the subsidy is treated as ordinary taxable income. In the qualified case, the employer may not be able to deduct the cost of the subsidy. On the other hand, with a qualified plan, the employee may be eligible for special capital gains tax treatment if he or she holds onto the stock until the later of (1) two years following the grant date, or (2) one year following the stock purchase.

In a recent Hewitt Associates survey of 100 ESPP sponsors, 70% used qualified plans and 30% used nonqualified plans. Of the 100 companies surveyed, only 3% of qualified plans had less than 10% of employees participating, while almost 40% of the nonqualified plans had participation rates below 10%. Despite these higher participation rates in qualified plans, many employers prefer nonqualified plans because qualified plans offer less significant employer tax deductions and are less flexible from a design and implementation perspective.

Qualified plan design restrictions include a requirement that, essentially, the plan needs to cover almost all U.S. employees of the company who meet certain minimum service requirements (except for more-than-5% owners, who must be excluded). There are limited exceptions; for example, foreign subsidiaries and employees in countries with laws that make ESPPs either illegal or impractical may be excluded. Also, union members may be excluded if this is negotiated separately with the union. In addition, all employees must be offered the same purchase rights, so the design cannot be structured to target certain classes of employees with favorable treatment. Nonqualified plans on the other hand, can be designed to deliver enhanced benefits to a very specific group of employees.

Perhaps even more troublesome for some employers is the requirement that a qualified plan must receive shareholder approval within 12 months of the plan's effective date. A nonqualified plan, on the other hand, does not need to be approved by shareholders. Some nonqualified plans are even designed to mimic a qualified plan in every feature short of seeking shareholder approval. In the Hewitt survey, almost half of the respondents with nonqualified plans did not obtain shareholder approval.

In either case, companies have adopted both qualified and nonqualified ESPPs in large number as a way of promoting stock ownership through a broad based employee population.

The Unrealized Potential of ESPPs

The sad truth is that many ESPPs are underused and undervalued by the very people whose behavior they're intended to influence. In terms of *perceived value,* they show up as the fourth or fifth most highly valued benefit by employees in most employee surveys (well behind medical benefits, vacation time, the 401(k) plans, and the subsidized company cafeteria). In many cases, that's well below management's expectations. As one benefit manager put it, "they're the redheaded, cross-eyed, freckle-faced stepchild of benefits."

What do employers expect in implementing an ESPP? Most look for broad participation across income levels and employment categories. Many would like employees to hold onto the shares they purchase for a significant period of time. In some cases, the sponsoring company views its ESPP as a relatively inexpensive way to deliver extra monetary rewards. In still other companies, the emphasis is on the ESPP as a focus for continuing economic education. Other organizations see the ESPP as a way of reinforcing the alignment of business goals and participant behavior.

Given this mix of goals and expectations, judging the "success" of an ESPP can be difficult. Many have settled on participation as the key success measure—how many employees are willing to put their own money on the line to buy their company's stock? In terms of participation rates, a successful ESPP might attract 50% to 70% of eligible employees. The highest participation level reported in the 1998 Hewitt survey was 80%. Conversely, the least "successful" plan had only 1% of employees participating.

Increasing Participation Rates: Some Considerations

Why are the ESPP participation rates in some companies far higher than in others? What's causing employees in one organization to "get in the game" while others sit on the sidelines? In an attempt to answer these questions and to pin down the success factors associated with ESPPs, we examined the data collected in the 1998 Hewitt Associates *Employee Stock Purchase Plan Survey*. This survey covered a broad range of questions relating to the design and administration of ESPPs at 100 U.S. companies. We concentrated on 30 companies with qualified ESPPs. Fifteen of those companies had exceptionally high participation rates; 15 had low participation rates. For convenience, we call them the "top 15" and the "bottom 15" respectively. We also looked at 10 nonqualified ESPPs (5 with high participation and 5 with very low participation).

From this data and our experience communicating and administering a variety of contributory benefit plans, we have developed a list of success factors, common pitfalls, and suggestions for the education and training associated with ESPPs. Some are obvious and might be labeled "no-brainers." Others are more subtle and judgmental. All are worth considering if you are installing or expanding an ESPP.

The Influence of Plan Design Features

Based on the plan experience of many companies, it is logical to assume that stock price performance is a significant influence on participation. Companies whose stock has enjoyed rapid appreciation should have more eligible employees in their plans and vice versa. Unfortunately, the data available on this particular aspect are incomplete and limited. Although probably true, this correlation needs future study.

Other "no-brainers" would seem to be certain plan design features. Intuitively, those plans that allow the most direct opportunity to gain economically should have higher participation rates. We examined the designs of the top 15 and the bottom 15 qualified plans and the features of the 10 nonqualified plans to identify the characteristics that seem to affect participation. Our focus centered on the three points described earlier—the employer subsidy, the purchase price date, and the accumulation period.

The Employer Subsidy   When reviewing the survey data, we noticed that the presence of a discount is more common than any other plan feature of qualified plans. Of the 70 companies surveyed that have qualified plans, only three did not provide at least a 5% discount. In fact, more than 80% of the respondents offer the maximum 15% discount allowed under Section 423. This almost universal use of the full 15% discount is in line with the data from the 1998 NASPP survey. In that survey, almost 83% of the 178 qualified plans provided the maximum 15% discount. In the Hewitt survey, 14 of the 15 top qualified plans provide the full 15% discount (one has no discount or match). At the other extreme, 10 of the 15 companies with the lowest participation rates provide the full 15% discount, and 4 of the remaining are at either 5% or 10% discounts. In other words, there is no correlation between the presence of the maximum discount and higher participation rates.

When we examine the *nonqualified* plans in the survey, we see more of a distinction between the top and bottom companies. Discounts and matches are much less common. Only 40% of the 30 nonqualified plans surveyed provided a match or a discount. However, three of the companies with the highest participation rates have some sort of match, while only one of the bottom five offers a subsidy, in the form of a 10% discount. While the number of companies in this group is small, it does seem reasonable to expect more employees to take advantage of a plan when there is a strong financial incentive, i.e., "free money," to do so.

Thus, it appears that the discount in a qualified plan design is more a cost of "entering the game" than a variation that distinguishes many plans. The nonqualified plan survey respondents in the Hewitt survey *with* a match or discount had participation rates that averaged 32%, compared to a 16% level for those companies *without* a match or discount. Our conclusion is that a match or discount may make a significant difference in terms of participation rates in nonqualified plans, but with qualified plans, other variables must also be at work.

Purchase Price Date   As we noted earlier, employees may also receive additional value from the program if the purchase price is tied to an earlier date than the end of the accumulation period, since it offers an opportunity for the purchase price to be lower than the current market price.

More than 70% of the qualified plans surveyed peg the purchase price off the *lower of* the market price at the beginning or end of the accumulation period. Of the top 15 companies in the 1998 Hewitt survey group, thirteen plans (87%) provide the maximum leverage on determining the purchase price by using the lesser of the beginning or end of period price. Slightly less than half of the bottom 15 use this feature. The remaining companies either use the end of period price or some average value. Nonqualified plans show a different picture. Most (67%) tie the purchase price to the market price at the end of the accumulation period. There are no observable differences between the best and the worst companies in the Hewitt survey. Our conclusion is that for qualified plans, the purchase price date seems to be a factor that influences or correlates with higher plan participation.

Accumulation Period   Most qualified plans in the 1998 Hewitt survey have an accumulation period of six months. The nonqualified plans in the survey are more likely to have a one-month accumulation period. The longer the accumulation period, the more the employee can benefit if the purchase price is based on the lower of beginning or end of-the purchase period.

For example, take a simple design. In this hypothetical plan, the purchase price is the lesser of the beginning of period and end of period market value, and there is no discount.

Let us assume that an employee contributes $3,000 during the year, the stock price is $10 at the beginning of the year, and the stock price *increases* 10% during the year (table 4-2).

Table 4-2. Illustrations of 6- and 12-Month Periods

	Accumulation Period	
	6 Months	12 Months
1. January 1 Market Price	$10.00	$10.00
June 30 Purchase Date:		
2. Market Price	$10.50	NA
3. Purchase Price	$10.00	NA
4. Employee Contributions for Period	$1,500	NA
5. Shares Purchased	150	NA
December 31 Purchase Date:		
6. Market Price	$11.00	$11.00
7. Purchase Price	$10.50	$10.00
8. Employee Contributions for Period	$1,500	$3,000
9. Shares Purchased	143	300
Cumulative Results:		
10. Total Shares Purchased	293	300
11. Market Value of Shares	$3,223	$3,300
12. Profit	$223	$300
13. Return on Investment	7.4%	10.0%

As these figures show, the plan with a 12-month purchase period provides an additional $77 in value to the participant (or 35 percent) by the end of the year. What is more, the vast majority (84%) of qualified plans surveyed allow employees to withdraw contributions *before* the end of the accumulation period. This gives participants extra protection against deteriorating stock prices and may help alleviate concern about participating.

In terms of accumulation periods, qualified plans with the highest participation rates show a marked difference from those with low participation rates. The top 15 have an average accumulation period of *twelve* months. In fact, only one of these companies uses a period of less than six months. Participation rates for the bottom 15 have an average accumulation period of only *seven* months; seven have periods of three months or less. Our conclusion: the value-adding impact of a longer accumulation period is significant. Despite the significant influence of plan characteristics on participation rates, however, certain other factors seem to be at work when we examine the top 15 versus the bottom 15 as well as at the top and bottom nonqualified plans.

Communication

One very manageable way to increase participation in a stock purchase plan is with a comprehensive communication campaign. Employees need to know what the plan is, how it works, how they can benefit it from it, and how they can affect the value of the stock they pruchase through the plan. Interviews with those who administer and operate ESPPs in both the top 15 and the bottom 15 demonstrate the importance of having high-volume, high-quality education and training associated with the plan.

The Hewitt survey results do not contain the data to examine plan participation in terms of education and training practices, but the value of effective descriptive materials and activities was mentioned as important by many survey respondents. Experience shows that effective education and training for employee stock purchase plans has certain definable characteristics. In approximate order of importance, they are:

- Plan effectively
- Recognize the challenge as an ongoing one
- Devote adequate resources
- Link to other related plans and policies
- Administer smoothly

- Build manager advocacy
- Test evolving approaches in process
- Strike the right balance between technical vs. engaging content

Effective Planning

The key to successful training and education for an ESPP is effective planning. All too often, planning is cursory. Someone says, "Let's send out a brochure with a cover memo from the CEO," and the planning process goes no further.

But an organized approach based on thoughtful discussion can make a tangible difference. An ESPP is the means to an end, not an end itself. ESPP companies typically want to achieve specific goals with their plan:

- Better alignment with shareholder interests
- Improved wealth-building opportunities for employees
- More employee ownership of the company
- Higher productivity
- Greater employee knowledge of the company's stock price movements
- More employee engagement or commitment to the company

In a good planning process, these broader contextual issues translate into *measurable criteria* that also shape the communication created for the plan. In other words, the objectives for the education and training behind an ESPP should be based on the purposes to be served by the plan itself.

More specifically, a handful of clear, well-stated objectives should be reduced to writing at the outset. One typical goal might be "to create understanding and buy-in that results in at least a 50% participation rate by the end of the year." Another might be to link the plan's communication approach to other initiatives designed to build an engaged, committed workforce. Key messages can be developed that tie to those goals and then worked into all the media and activities associated with the campaign. Those messages should explain the "why" as well as the "what."

An Ongoing Challenge

Experience shows that companies who view their communication challenges as continuing are more successful than those who focus on communication as a one-time event.

Advertising research tells us that it takes seven repetitions of a message to create an action-response on the part of someone who isn't predisposed to the product. Educational psychologists speak of multiple "learning styles," which suggests the need for a program that incorporates a variety of media and activities. Some people learn best by "doing," which implies exercises and interaction. Some learn best from the printed page; others through face-to-face discussion, and so on.

Regular reminders, reinforcement, and repetition are key success factors, and the most effective campaigns are planned that way. After a lukewarm response to the launch of its ESPP, a major East Coast bank embarked on a carefully planned two-year campaign to build participation to the level specified in its objectives. Using a combination of employee meetings, newsletters, posters and other internal media, the bank increased participation from a barely acceptable 12% to a more than respectable 39% in two years. But the process demanded time and resources. In influencing employee behavior, there are few shortcuts.

It is interesting to note that the employees who participated in the ESPP mentioned above stayed with their employer longer. Turnover was approximately 11.5% among plan participants but more than 19% for non-participants. In addition, over one-half the participants track the company's stock price regularly, compared with only 20% for those employees who do not take advantage of the ESPP. Keep in mind that these correlations are just that. Cause and effect are subject to further study.

Adequate Resources

Devoting too few resources to the education and training for an ESPP is a common failing. Some consumer products sell for $3 but cost only 20 cents to produce. The difference of $2.80 is the cost of bringing that product to market. Similarly, the cost of bringing an ESPP to its employee "customers" needs to be viewed as a significant investment.

For a mid-sized employer with 10,000 to 30,000 potential participants, an initial ESPP communication budget of $5 to $10 per employee is not uncommon. Ongoing yearly communication costs close to those levels may be appropriate to maintain the visibility required to meet the participation objectives defined for the plan.

Some of the common elements of the most effective campaigns include:

- Clear, straightforward writing that uses simple terms and minimal use of technical jargon

- Professional and engaging graphics

- Content tied to employee behavior (e.g., "here's how these plan features might affect your participation decisions")

- Explicit management endorsement of the plan

Unrelenting pressure to suppress the cost of effective training and education comes at a price. The price of cutting costs on communicating the plan can be an undersubscribed, passive plan that has no visible impact on the sponsoring company.

Linkages

Stated or unstated, the objectives behind the plan often encompass issues of employee motivation, productivity, wealth building, and behavior. The same is true for other human resource programs and policies, such as performance management systems, management incentive systems, and career development plans. Often, an ESPP will be one part of a larger strategy to accomplish these larger, more long-term goals.

Effective ESPP education and training refers to and reinforces these strategic links so that their influences compound each other. Look for commonality, similar vocabulary, and related characteristics. Make those connections explicit at every opportunity. For example, one successful campaign bundled all the stock ownership vehicles sponsored by the company under one overall theme of ownership and combined achievement. Another included the value of all company stock owned by the employee on the individualized total compensation statement.

Smooth Administration

The effect of administration on plan success is difficult to measure. While poor administration is easy to recognize, the mediocre often blends into the background. From an employee perspective, how easy is the sign-up process? What standards of performance have been established for the record keeper and/or brokerage organization associated with the plan? How easy is it for employees to get accurate, consistent answers to their questions? (Editor's note: These issues are discussed in greater detail in Chapter 3, "Administering an ESPP.")

Manager Advocacy

No company seeking to establish or revitalize an ESPP should ignore the powerful influence of managers in determining success. For most employees, their immediate manager is a key influence on attitude and behavior. A negative or neutral manager can drag down the best-planned, most professionally prepared campaign.

Building manager advocacy can be accomplished in a variety of ways. Simply distributing advance copies of material that is soon to be sent to employees can make a difference. Recognizing first-line management as a singular audience can establish the foundation for a clear role in the communication process.

Other commonly used techniques include manager briefings on plan operations, management newsletter feature stories, distribution of work-unit participation statistics (and mapping them to changes in stock price), and suggested talking points for use in informal work group meetings.

Testing

There are few universal success factors in education and training. What works in one environment can flop in another. Testing an emerging ESPP communication approach with focus groups or with an ad hoc group of non-HR employees can have a big payoff. It can "bullet proof" the implementation process. For example, one company was near the final approval stages for an ESPP presentation to be used in employee meetings. As an afterthought, someone suggested previewing the semi-finished materials with a quickly assembled group of employees. After the presenter finished, most employees commented favorably. Finally, one employee mustered up the courage to ask, "Uh . . . it sounds fine. But . . . what exactly is stock?" That one comment resulted in new presentation content and a much more successful launch.

Strike a Balance

Technically, an ESPP is an offering of registered securities. As such, it is subject to the Securities and Exchange Commission's disclosure requirements. Most of these requirements are taken care of (in public companies) by issuing an up-to-date stock prospectus and the company's annual report. But for many employees, the language and approaches used in such documents is far from engaging. And it certainly shouldn't set the tone for the rest of the campaign. There needs to be an effective *balance* between technical content and engaging context.

Effective education and training materials use simple vocabulary, lots of examples, relevant analogies, pictures or graphics that tell a story and appealing design. Completeness and accuracy should be primary concerns. But in the interests of plan success, no one should stop there.

Closing Thoughts

No one ESPP design or communication approach suits every company's needs. Stock price performance, as well as certain plan design features, such as purchase discounts, employer subsidies, and accumulation periods are among the factors that are correlated with plan participation rates. But stock performance and plan design are only some of the factors at work, and it may be that plan participation is viewed as a key measure of success primarily because it's easy to determine. Regardless, practical experience places strong emphasis on the importance of education and training. Whatever goals stand behind an ESPP, it is hard to imagine achieving any of them without effective communication.

CHAPTER 5

Recent Research and Case Studies

Ed Carberry and Ryan Weeden

To establish an equity-based compensation plan that complies with various laws and regulations and best meets corporate objectives, it is essential to have a thorough understanding of the key technical issues relating to tax, accounting, securities, and other regulatory areas. Often, however, this information overshadows the lessons offered by the experiences of companies that have implemented plans. What do employee stock purchase plans look like in actual companies? This chapter reviews the research about how companies are designing and operating their ESPPs and provides case studies of ESPPs in six companies that have high participation rates in their plans.

An Overview of Plan Design Features

Although ESPPs provide some flexibility in terms of many plan design features, the basic design issues are not as complex as those relating to stock option plans or ESOPs. In fact, the research shows there is little variation in plan design from plan to plan.

In most ESPPs, employees purchase shares on predetermined dates with their own funds, which in most plans they accumulate through payroll deductions. In many plans, employees can purchase shares at a discount.

In general, companies do have some flexibility in deciding who will be eligible to purchase shares, the discount on the purchase price, the date on which the purchase price is set, the length of the offering period, the maximum number of shares employees can purchase, and the length of the offering period. Companies also can establish their own guidelines about when employees can enroll in a plan, whether employees can make withdrawals or additional contributions, and the definition of eligible compensation for determining deferrals.

Limitations Imposed by Section 423

With nonqualified purchase plans, there are few restrictions on plan design. Section 423 plans, however, must comply with more stringent requirements to qualify for different tax treatment, and hence have less flexibility. For example, with a 423 plan, most employees must be given the opportunity to purchase stock, although certain employees can be excluded, such as those who have worked at the company for less than two years, employees who work less that 20 hours per week, employees who work less than 5 months in a calendar year, and highly compensated employees as defined in Section 414(q) of the Internal Revenue Code. If giving most employees the opportunity to purchase stock is not a goal for your company, a 423 plan probably does not make sense.

Section 423 plans also limit the amount of stock an employee can purchase through the plan in any one calendar year to $25,000 of the fair market value at the time of grant. Plans meet this requirement through a number of methods. Some simply monitor the share acquisition of employees and cap purchases at the maximum limit, while other plans specify the maximum percentage of pay an employee can defer. A plan might specify a maximum salary deferral of 15% of pay per year; however, most employees will not choose the maximum deferral.

In a 423 plan, the purchase price can not be less than 85% of the fair market value on the date of grant or on the date of purchase. The offering period cannot be longer than 27 months, unless the purchase price is based on the fair market value at the time of purchase. If this is the case, then the offering period can be as long as 5 years.

While these restrictions do impose limitations on how a company will design its 423 plan, rarely are these limitations onerous from the company's perspective. Most companies establish these plans simply as a way to provide employees with an opportunity to purchase stock, and most 423 plans have very similar plan design features. The most common reason why companies manipulate certain plan design features is to increase participation in the plan. As Chapter 4, "Getting the Most Out of Your ESPP," details, there are certain plan design features that can help increase participation rates, such as the size of the discount (making it as large as possible), the length of the offering period (making it as long as possible), the presence of a look-back feature, and the availability of favorable tax treatment (using a tax-qualified 423 plan). Of course, not every company structures its plan to solely maximize participation rates; companies must also balance shareholder concerns about dilution, philosophical issues relating to "giving away" too much to employees, and the need or desire to have a corporate tax deduction available on the gains employees receive from purchases.

Recent Research on ESPPs

So how are companies designing their plans? The answer, as with most things in trend analysis, is a conditional "it depends." The research that has been conducted to date provides useful information, but is far from comprehensive. No research, for example, has looked at plan design characteristics by company size, annual sales, or industry group. There are also no studies that examine plan participation rates in detail. In this section we review four surveys:

1. *Employee Stock Purchase Trends: A Survey of Equity Compensation Professionals* (ShareData, 1995): ShareData, a provider of stock plan administration software, conducted a survey of approximately 100 of its customers regarding the design and operation of their stock purchase plans. In the ShareData survey, almost 80% of the respondents were located in the western United States, and most companies represented high-tech, software, and communications industries.

2. *1996 Stock Plan and Design and Survey Report* (National Association of Stock Plan Professionals [NASPP], 1997): NASPP, a trade association, conducted an extensive survey of approximately 400 of its members, looking at equity compensation plan design and administration issues for a variety of plans. The survey includes a brief section on ESPP practices. The NASPP surveys looked at a diverse group of companies in terms of size, industry, and geography; all were public.

3. *1998 Stock Plan Design and Administration Survey* (National Association of Stock Plan Professionals, 1999): This is a follow-up to the survey discussed above.

4. *Survey Findings: Employee Stock Purchase Plans* (Hewitt Associates, 1998): Hewitt Associates, a large international human resources consulting firm, conducted a study of companies with nonqualified and qualified stock purchase plans. The Hewitt survey details the ESPP practices of 100 companies that range in size from less than 500 employees to over 50,000. The Hewitt survey is the most extensive one that has been done to date.

The remainder of this section discusses the findings of this research, broken down by specific plan design and operational issues. All data on nonqualified plans includes open-market purchase plans.

Primary Plan Design Features

Prevalence of ESPPs   One of the most common questions regarding any form of equity compensation is the number of companies using a particular practice. No research has measured the number of companies using ESPPs. Both the ShareData and Hewitt surveys looked exclusively at companies with ESPPs. NASPP's samples were more general, although most of the responding companies had some form of stock based compensation. In the 1996 NASPP survey, 211 companies (54%) had some form of ESPP. The 1998 NASPP survey found that 235 companies (59.5%) of companies had some form of ESPP for their U.S.-based employees, and 44% of companies with non-U.S.-based employees had an ESPP for these employees.

Qualified vs. Nonqualified Plans According to the 1996 NASPP survey, 57% of the companies with any type of stock purchase plan for U.S.-based employees had a 423 plan and 43% had a nonqualified plan. For the 1998 survey, these percentages were 75% and 27%, respectively. For 112 companies, including those non-U.S.-based employees in the 1998 survey, these percentages were 74% and 29%, respectively. (Note that for all of these distributions, some companies may have more than one type of plan.)

The Hewitt survey found that 70% of respondents use Section 423 plans, while the remaining 30% use nonqualified plans. In the ShareData survey, 99% of the respondents had a 423 plan. Although it is not possible to accurately state the ratio of 423 to nonqualified plans from these figures, 423 plans appear to be the most popular type of ESPP.

Some multinational companies are extending their 423 plans to employees in other countries. Because the tax benefits associated with 423 plans are only applicable to U.S.-based employees, we suspect that multinational companies are doing this to maintain a consistent global employee stock plan, streamline communication issues, and simplify administration.

Participation Rates The Hewitt survey was the only one to look at the percentages for employees that were actually purchasing stock through the plans. For 423 plans, Hewitt found that 44% of the companies had 25% or less of eligible employees purchasing stock. Thirty-eight percent of the respondents reported that between 26% and 50% purchase stock; and 18% had more than 50%. For nonqualified plans, these percentages were 62%, 28%, and 10%, respectively. So although 423 plans have more employees participating than in nonqualified plans, participation rates in 423 plans are still low, with over three-quarters of the companies reporting that fewer than half of their employees participate in the plan.

Offering Periods   The offering period is the length of time during which an employee can purchase stock. Some plans will have one purchase date at the end of the offering period. Other plans allow for multiple purchases at specific times (e.g., every 6 months) within the period. If the plan has a look-back feature, the purchase price is set by taking the lower of the fair market value at the date of grant and the fair market value at the beginning of the offering period. This period of time is also sometimes referred to as an "enrollment period" or "accumulation period." The varied terminology for the same thing can be confusing. We will use the term "offering period."

The length of an offering period can affect the outcome of the plan. Longer offering periods, providing they use a "look-back" feature, can convey a greater benefit to employees because the potential purchase price is locked in at an earlier date. Shorter offering periods, on the other hand, allow employees greater flexibility in enrolling for shorter periods of time, such as when they believe they can afford it or when they are optimistic about the stock price, for example.

Table 5-1 summarizes the data about offering periods from the four surveys, indicating that in Section 423 plans, although there is variation in the length of offering period, most are periods are between 3 and 12 months. In nonqualified plans, offering periods are frequently shorter. The numbers for nonqualified plans include open-market plans.

Purchase Discount and Stock Price Application   The discount provided to employees on the purchase price of the stock varies considerably by the type of plan. Section 423 plans

Table 5-1. Offering Periods

	ShareData	Hewitt		NASPP (1996)		NASPP (1998)	
	Section 423	Section 423	Non-qualified	Section 423	Non-qualified	Section 423	Non-qualified
1 month	0%	7%	47%	N/A	N/A	10%	44%
3 months	0%	20%	13%	14%	23%	24%	13%
6 months	47%	36%	3%	36%	2.5%	47%	13%
12 months	12%	17%	13%	27%	10%	13%	8%
24 months	28%	7%	0%	12%	5%	2%	0%
Other	13%	13%	24%	14%	59%	4%	23%

tend to have larger discounts than nonqualified plans, and most 423 plans provide the maximum 15% discount. ShareData, for example, found that 98% of the companies it surveyed offer a 15% discount. The 1996 NASPP survey also found 15% to be the most typical discount in a 423 plan. The 1998 survey found that 83% of the 423 plans offered a 15% discount. In the Hewitt survey, this percentage was 86%.

A lower percentage of nonqualified plans offer a discount. For nonqualified plans, including open-market purchase plans, the 1998 NASPP survey found that 23% of these plans offered a 15% discount, and 50% no discount. Hewitt found that 73% of nonqualified plans provided no discount, and 17% provided a 15% discount.

Table 5-2 indicates that in terms of the date at which the purchase price is set, most 423 plans have a "look-back feature," which allows the purchase price to set at the lower of the fair market value of the stock at either the beginning of the offering period or on the date of purchase. Look-back features are less common in nonqualified ESPPs.

Other Issues

The Hewitt survey was the most extensive and included information on other issues relating to plan design and operation.

Table 5-2. Establishment of Purchase Price

	ShareData	Hewitt		NASPP (1996)		NASPP (1998)	
	Section 423	Section 423	Non-qualified	Section 423	Non-qualified	Section 423	Non-qualified
"Look-back" feature	91%	73%	6%	69%	20%	81%	33%
End of period	7%	10%	67%	11%	20%	9.5%	30%
Other*	2%	17%	27%	.8%	60%	9.5%	37%

*Includes "average for accumulation period," "closing price on certain dates," or "price at beginning of offering period"

Interim Purchases Interim purchases allow employees to purchase stock at predetermined times during the offering period instead of only at the end of the offering period. This gives employees in a long-term offering period the opportunity to "dollar-cost average" the purchases of stock at predetermined periods of time. Interim purchases are most often allowed in plans with offering periods of 12 to 24 months and occur usually at 3- to 6-month intervals. Fewer than 20% of respondents in the Hewitt survey allow interim purchases.

Direct Cash Contributions Hewitt's study found that only 10% of companies with 423 plans allow employees to make additional contributions of their own funds to purchase stock through an ESPP. This practice is more common in companies with nonqualified plans, as 60% allow their employees to make cash contributions to purchase stock through the ESPP. Most of the companies that allow direct cash contributions do so without restriction to the amount of money; however, some limit the dollar amount or the number of shares that can be purchased with contributed money.

Early Withdrawal Due to unforeseen circumstances, employees may need to withdraw from making deferrals to the plan. Most companies (84%) with 423 plans in the Hewitt study allow employees to withdraw before the end of an offering period. Approximately half the companies with nonqualified plans allow employees to withdraw before the end of the offering period. When permitted, there is typically no penalty for making withdrawals from the plan, and participants are refunded their prior contributions upon withdrawal.

Employee Stock Holding and Tracking A key issue in terms of ESPPs promoting long-term employee stock ownership is how long employees hold onto their shares after they have purchased them. It is difficult to determine exactly what employees are doing in this area as comprehensive data is scarce.

Hewitt's study found that regardless of the type of plan, the holding practices are about the same. For both types of plans, 15% of the companies reported that employees do not hold or sell shortly after purchase. Five percent reported that employees hold for a year or two. Twenty-two percent reported that employees hold for several years or more, and 29% reported that it varies by types of employee. The rest did not know. The common belief is that employees do not hold onto their shares long after purchase. Hewitt's figures do not confirm this and suggest that there is more widespread variation in holding practices. Hewitt also found that few companies build any kind of stock retention incentives into their purchase plans. Fourteen percent had a minimum holding period for a stock purchase; only 4% impose a penalty on employees for an immediate sale after a purchase; and only 1% provide additional incentives for holding stock.

Payment of Brokerage Fees The participants in ESPPs almost always pay the brokerage fees associated with the purchase and sale of stock through the plan. Hewitt's survey found that 90% of companies with Section 423 plans and 97% of companies with nonqualified ESPPs make the participant pay the associated brokerage fees.

Plan Administration and Communication Hewitt also looked at plan administration and communication. It found that half the companies use a broker or transfer agent to handle the record keeping, while 41% do most of the administration in-house. Hewitt also found that over three-quarters of the companies with 423 plans track disqualifying dispositions.

Hewitt found that written material is the most popular medium for communicating the plan, with a majority of companies using this mechanism at the time the plan is adopted, when an employee is hired, or annually. Twenty-four percent of the companies conducted one-on-one counseling about the plan for new employees, and 20% used the Internet or an intranet on an ongoing basis.

Trends and Unanswered Questions

Although the research conducted so far is far from comprehensive, it suggests some trends. The research shows that Section 423 plans are the most popular type of employee stock purchase plan. The studies reviewed here also suggest that the largest variations in terms of plan design, such as the length of the offering, the discount, and the presence of a look-back feature, occur between 423 and nonqualified plans, and that there is a great deal of consistency in the design features of 423 plans. For example, most 423 plans have a look-back feature, offer the maximum 15% discount, and have an offering period between 3 and 12 months. Finally, the only survey to look at plan participation rates, the Hewitt study, indicates that these most plans do not have a majority of employees purchasing stock.

There remain a number of unanswered questions about stock purchase plans. A more thorough study is needed that examines plan design features by company size, industry group, and region. Furthermore, the key issues of participation rates, employee stock holding practices, and the relationship between plan design, communication, and participation rates need to be explored in much greater detail.

Case Studies

While the research summarized above provides us with an informative picture of how companies are designing their purchase plans, it also is useful to take a closer look how individual companies design their plans. The following case studies provide information on six companies with 423 plans. We chose these companies because all of them have relatively high percentages of employees purchasing stock through their plans, from 40% to over 70%. The intention is to give the reader a look at how these plans work in actual companies, how they are received by employees, how they are administered and communicated, and the effects the plans have had on employees and the company. The case studies are based on a brief survey sent to the companies. Any quotes are taken directly from the survey and are attributable to the survey respondent. Plan information was current at the time of collection, January 2000. The information in each description contains the following:

- *General information about the company:* When it was founded, industry, location, the number of employees, and annual sales.

- Details about the stock purchase plan, including:

  — *Start:* When the plan was first implemented.

  — *Purchase price:* The price at which employees are able to purchase stock.

  — *Discount:* The discount, if any, applied to the purchase price.

  — *Offering period:* The length of the period during which employees are able to purchase stock.

  — *Purchase dates:* The number and frequency of dates that employees can actually purchase stock during the offering period.

  — *Maximum number of shares/maximum deferral amount:* The maximum number of shares that employees can purchase on the purchase dates or the maximum percentage of salary that employees can defer each pay period to accumulate for stock purchases.

  — *Other features:* Miscellaneous plan design characteristics, such as how salary is defined for calculating the deferrals, whether or not employees can make additional contributions, and whether employees can make withdrawals from their accounts before the purchase date.

- *Participation:* Describes eligibility for the plan, how many employees purchase stock through plan, and how long employees hold onto the stock after purchase.

- *Administration:* How the company administers the plan and who is involved with these tasks.

- *Communication:* The methods the company uses to communicate the purchase plan to employees and the perceived effectiveness of these methods.

- *Employee participation:* Any formal structures the company uses to share ideas and information with employees and get employees more involved in decision-making within the company.

- *Effects:* Impacts the plan has had on employee attitudes and/or company performance.

- *Advice:* survey respondents provide advice for companies that are considering implementing a stock purchase plan or companies that are looking to increase participation rates in their stock purchase programs.

E*TRADE

Founded: 1982

Industry: On-line investing services

Location: Menlo Park, CA

Employees: 1,700

Annual sales: $1.01 billion (for the nine months ending June 2000)

Other equity compensation plans: stock options

Plan Details

Start: Created in 1996 as an employee benefit

Purchase price: Lower of (1) fair market value at beginning of the offering period or (2) the average of the high/low of fair market value during the offering period

Discount: 15%

Offering period: 2 years

Purchase dates: every 6 months

Type of stock: common stock

Maximum deferral: 10% of pay

Other features: Only base pay is used for the deduction amount. Employees cannot make additional contributions, but can make withdrawals

Participation

All employees are eligible to participate after six months of employment. Approximately 60% purchase stock through the plan. In terms of which employees participate, 51% of employees in the lowest third in (terms of salary) purchase stock; 69% of the middle third; and 82% of the top third. The participation rate has increased in the last five years. On average, employees hold onto the stock for one year after purchase.

Administration

E*TRADE administers the plan in-house using a commercial software package. Two people in HR and payroll handle administration. They track disqualifying dispositions and do not have a captive broker.

Communication

E*TRADE uses written materials, meetings, email, and an intranet site to communicate the plan. They have found that meetings and the intranet have been the most effective because people at all levels can access this information.

Employee Participation

The company holds regular meetings with employees to discuss company performance, strategy, and goals, as well as regular meetings to contribute input about jobs as well as meetings to allow employees to provide input to upper management.

Effects

The plan is viewed both as a long-term and short-term incentive. People are more focused on results.

Advice

"Make it attractive, provide a discount, comprehensive communication, supplement to 401(k) plan and stock option plan."

Genzyme Corporation

Founded: 1981

Industry: Biotechnology

Location: Cambridge, MA

Employees: 3,800

Annual Sales: $709 million

Other forms of equity compensation: stock options, 401(k) with company stock as an investment

Plan Details

Purchase price: fair market value on the purchase date or beginning of offering period, whichever is lower

Discount: 15%

Offering period: 24 months

Purchase dates: 8 (quarterly)

Type of stock offered: common

Maximum number of shares/maximum deferral: calculated for the total pool available, not on individual level. This is a percentage of the total number of outstanding shares from the previous fiscal year.

Other features: Overtime is included as part of pay for the payroll deduction calculation. Employees can make withdrawals before the end of the offering period.

Plan Participation

All employees are eligible to participate, and over 45% purchase stock. This percentage has increased in the last five years. Small group meetings to communicate the plan have worked very well to increase this percentage. About half of the stock purchased by employees is sold less than a year after purchase.

Administration

Five people in the shareholder relations department administer the plan in-house. They use a commercial software package and track disqualifying dispositions.

Communication

Genzyme communicates the plan through written materials and meetings. The latter have been the most effective. In the meetings, employees get to ask questions and develop a better understanding of plan benefits in an interactive environment. Written materials contain many concrete examples.

Effects of the Plan

About half of the employees view the purchase plan as a long-term incentive. The plan has made employees take a more active interest in the performance of the company.

Advice

"When communicating, give lots of examples and explain the issues clearly."

National Semiconductor Corporation

Founded: May 27, 1959

Industry: Semiconductor manufacturing

Location: Headquartered in Santa Clara, California with 20-plus offices worldwide

Employees: 10,500

Annual Sales: $2.14 billion

Other types of equity compensation plans: bonus plan for key employees, and a success-sharing plan for all other personnel. National Semiconductor has a 401(k) plan through which employees can also invest in company stock.

Plan Details

Start: the ESPP was established in 1977. Management thought it would help the company stay ahead of the industry, as well as keep employees interested.

Purchase price: The purchase price is the lower of fair market value on the first or last day of the quarter.

Discount: 15%

Purchase dates: 4, offered every 3 months.

Type of stock offered: Common

Maximum purchase amount/deferral: 10% of eligible compensation.

Other features: Everything except bonuses is included in the base pay calculation, including commission, overtime, and lead premiums. Basically, they use the same definition of compensation used to define eligible compensation for 40l(k) plans. An autosell feature is built into the plan through the captive brokers. Employees can sell their stock as soon as they purchase it, and the money will be in their accounts the next day. About one-third take advantage of this feature.

Plan Participation

The stock purchase plan is for U.S. employees only, although there is a separate look-alike plan for offshore employees. All employees are eligible, and there is no minimum service requirement. All employees who are employed by the 15th of the month before the start of the quarter can participate. Forty-five percent of all employees purchase stock, with about 12% of offshore employees participating in the look-alike plan. Participation has remained steady. The company does not track how long employees hold the stock.

Administration

Four people in the stock administration department administer the plan in-house. The head of the department reports directly to the general counsel. They do not use a commercial software package to aid with administration. They track disqualifying dispositions through two captive brokers and through transfer agent reports.

Communication

National does a significant amount of education about how the stock purchase plan works. Monthly seminars are conducted at the company's Santa Clara headquarters. Other locations have annual educational programs. National distributes a booklet that explains the plan and a prospectus for new hires. The company also uses e-mail. Stock plan administrator Sandy Miller says that the personal contact people have with her during the training/educational seminars has been the most effective means of communication. "People like to know who they are dealing with," she says.

Employee Participation

Employees can attend free training courses on basis business concepts through their credit union. There are regular meetings to discuss company performance, strategy, and goals; to contribute input about jobs and the work environment; and to contribute input to upper management. One such event is the quarterly open communication meeting in which employees get to ask the CEO questions. Employees also work in self-managing work teams.

Impacts

Miller does not think the plan has affected employee behavior as much as management would have liked. Employee attitudes vary with the price of the stock, which is fairly volatile. She thinks the overall impact has been neutral, but it does make employees aware of what the stock price is and how it's doing on the market.

Advice

"Make it as simple as possible and communicate it well. The more you talk about it, the more interested employees will be."

Western Digital Corporation

Founded: 1970

Industry: Disk drives

Location: Irvine, CA

Employees: 10,390

Annual Sales: $1.96 billion

Other equity compensation: stock options, 401(k) with stock as a match

Plan Details

Start: Plan was established in 1994 to provide an incentive for present and future employees to acquire a proprietary interest in the company through the purchase of common stock.

Purchase price: Price at purchase or beginning of period, whichever is lower

Discount: 15%

Offering period: 24 months

Purchase dates: every 6 months

Type of stock: common

Maximum deferral amount: 10% of pay

Other features: Compensation calculation for the deduction amount is based on regular salary, including commission, bonuses, and overtime. Employees cannot make additional contributions, but can make withdrawals before the end of the offering period.

Participation

All employees are eligible and must be employed on the enrollment date. About 40% of employees participate: 20% of employees in the bottom third (in terms of pay); 40% of the middle third; and 60% of the top third. This percentage has increased in the last 5 years. On average, most employees do not hold onto their shares after purchase.

Administration

Western Digital administers the plan in house, using a commercial software package. It has one and a half full-time employees in the legal and HR departments handling administration. Captive broker reports the sales monthly in order to track disqualifying dispositions.

Communication

Western Digital uses written materials, employee meetings, email, an interactive voice response system, and an intranet to communicate the plan. The most effective method has been word of mouth. There is heavy promotion of the plan in the month prior to the beginning of the offering period. In the week before, presentations are conducted on the plan at all locations.

Employee Participation

Western Digital conducts education and training on basic business concepts for employees. The company also shares financial information and gives employees regular opportunities to contribute input about jobs. The company also has self-managing work teams.

Advice

"Thorough education of employees is very important. They must understand the risks."

ABC Company

Founded: 1977
Industry: Software
Employees: 300
Annual Sales: $38 million
Other types of equity compensation plans: stock options

Plan Details

Start: The 423 plan was established in May 1996. The company was going public at the time.

Purchase price: Lesser of 85% of price at first date of quarter or the last date of quarter.

Discount: 15%

Offering period: 3 months

Purchase dates: 4 annually

Type of stock offered: common, the only class of stock offered by the company.

Maximum deferral: Employees cannot spend more than 25% of base pay in each purchase period.

Other features: Commission and overtime are not included in the payroll deduction calculation. Employees are not allowed to make additional contributions, but they can make withdrawals from the plan before the end of the offering period.

Plan Participation

All employees are eligible, and there is no minimum requirement for service. The overall participation rate is around 40%, with fairly even representation through all salary levels. The participation rate has stayed relatively level since the program began.

Administration

One person in the accounting department, who does not use a commercial software package, administers the plan in-house. Disqualifying dispositions are not tracked, and the company does not have a captive broker.

Communication

The company uses written materials, e-mail, an intranet, and verbal messages to communicate information about the plan to employees. Every new employee is given a 15-to 20-minute presentation about the plan details. These meetings have been the most effective way to educate people about the plan.

Employee Participation

The company shares financial information with employees, conducts regular meetings to discuss company performance, strategy, and goals, and gives employees opportunities to contribute input about their jobs or work environment. It also provides employees with opportunities to talk with upper management and the board.

Impacts

The plan has been effective in getting people to feel like owners, and employees do view it as a positive incentive to work harder and stay with the company. Employees "view it as a nice benefit. It aligns what they do with the interests of the shareholders."

Advice

"Take advantage of what is allowed by the SEC and IRS to provide employees with the best benefits you can and spend time when employees first start to communicate how the plan works and how it is a benefit to them—to get them familiar with it."

XYZ Company

Founded: 1983
Industry: Computer hardware
Employees: 2,510
Annual Sales: $800 million
Other types of equity compensation plans: stock options

Plan Details

Start: the 423 plan was established in 1987 with the goal of attracting and retaining employees and creating long-term employee shareholders.

Purchase price: Lesser of 85% of price at first date of quarter or the last date of quarter.

Discount: 15%

Offering period: 18 months

Purchase dates: 6, every 3 months. Employees can buy a maximum of 1,666 shares on each purchase date.

Type of stock offered: common

Holding period: an average of 6 months

Other features: Commission and overtime are included in the payroll deduction calculation. Employees are not allowed to make additional contribution, but they can make withdrawals from the plan before the end of the offering period.

Plan Participation

Everyone who works at least 20 hours week is eligible. Seventy-one percent of all employees buy stock, and this rate has gone up over the past five years. The stock plan administrator attributes these changes to the frequency of the purchase dates. Also, the implementation of an online, captive broker has made the facilitation of transactions easier.

Administration

One person in the accounting department, who does not use a commercial software package, administers the plan in-house.

Communication

The company uses written materials, an intranet, and e-mail to communicate information about the plan to employees. E-mail has been the most effective. The stock administration manager thinks this is because people are more likely to read something sent directly to them than they are to search a Web site for information. Pretty much any information employees want about the plan is available through the company's intranet. Employees are asked to attend regular meetings to discuss company performance, strategy, or goals.

Impacts

The company's stock administrator says that although employees view the stock purchase plan as a short-term incentive, it has been effective in getting them to feel like owners. When the stock is doing well, she says, people become more enthusiastic and motivated.

Advice

"Make sure the plan is favorable to people at all income levels."

About the Authors

Barbara A. Baksa

Barbara A. Baksa, CEP, is the manager of industry relations for E*TRADE Business Solutions. She serves as a spokesperson and subject matter expert for E*TRADE Business Solutions and is a frequent speaker on equity compensation-related topics. Ms. Baksa is responsible for conducting the E*TRADE Business Solutions seminar series covering the tax, accounting, and securities law treatment of equity compensation. In addition to her external role, Barbara's responsibilities include monitoring new developments in the equity compensation arena, advising on compliance issues related to current and new product developments, and responding to regulatory and industry-related questions that arise during the course of business. Barbara began her career with ShareData (now E*TRADE Business Solutions) over six years ago. Barbara has a B.A. in English from the University of Iowa and is a Certified Equity Professional.

Ed Carberry

Ed Carberry is a project director at the National Center for Employee Ownership (NCEO) and serves on the NCEO's board of directors. At the NCEO, he writes and edits publications, conducts research, and facilitates educational workshops on various topics relating to employee ownership. He is the author of *Corporate Governance in Employee Ownership Companies* (NCEO, 1996); a coauthor of *Current Practices in Stock Option Plan Design* (NCEO, 1998), *The Stock Options Book*, 3rd ed. (NCEO, 1999), and *Theory O: Creating an Ownership Style of Management*, 5th ed. (NCEO, 1999); and the editor of *Communicating Stock Options* (NCEO, 1999). He also has authored many articles on employee ownership for business and trade publications. Mr. Carberry holds a B.A. degree from Bates College in Lewiston, Maine.

Joseph M. Lazur

Joseph M. Lazur is a consulting actuary with Hewitt Associates LLC and a member of Hewitt's Ownership Network. He is a Fellow of the Society of Actuaries, an Enrolled Actuary, and a member of the American Academy of Actuaries. Joe splits his time between consulting on traditional defined benefit plans and helping companies understand the financial impact of adopting broad-based ownership programs. He has worked with both public and private companies considering ESPPs, ESOPs, and broad-based stock option plans. Joe holds a B.A. degree in mathematics *cum laude* from Cornell University and an M.S. degree in mathematics from the University of Michigan.

Donna Lowe

Donna Lowe, CPA, JD, is a senior manager at Deloitte & Touche LLP who provides compensation and employee benefits consulting to variety of clients. She has extensive experience in employee benefit plans and stock-based compensation arrangements and is a frequent speaker and author on stock-based compensation issues. Donna received her B.S. degree from Indiana University School of Business with majors in accounting and finance. She received her Doctorate of Jurisprudence from the Indiana University School of Law-Indianapolis. She is licensed as both a CPA and an attorney in Texas.

Paul W. Rangecroft

Paul W. Rangecroft is a consulting actuary with Hewitt Associates LLC. He is a Fellow of the Society of Actuaries, an Enrolled Actuary, and a member of the American Academy of Actuaries. He consults on the design and financial analysis of traditional defined benefit plans as well as broad-based employee ownership programs such as ESPPs and ESOPs. Paul earned a B.S. degree in mathematics and M.S. degree in statistics, both from the University of Kent at Canterbury in England.

Scott Rodrick

Scott Rodrick is a writer, editor, desktop publisher, and Web developer at the NCEO. He edits the *Journal of Employee Ownership Law and Finance* and also created and maintains the NCEO's Web site at *www.nceo.org.* Mr. Rodrick is the author of the booklet *An Introduction to ESOPs* (NCEO, rev. 3rd ed. 2000), the editor and/or coauthor of many other NCEO publications, such as *Leveraged ESOPs and Employee Buyouts,* and the coeditor of *Employee Stock Ownership Plans* (Harcourt Professional Publishing, 1996, 1999). He served at the U.S. Department of Labor as an attorney-advisor before coming to the NCEO. Before law school, he received a B.A. from U.C. Davis and an M.A. from UCLA.

Albert Schlachtmeyer

Albert Schlachtmeyer is a former owner of Hewitt Associates and has served as the firm's global practice leader for communication services. Now based in Washington, D.C., Mr. Schlachtmeyer's academic background includes an undergraduate degree in Radio, TV and Film from Northwestern University as well as graduate MBA work at Northwestern's Kellogg School of Business. He is a regular contributor to general business and professional publications as well as a featured speaker at such forums as the American Management Association, WorldatWork, the Society for Administrative Management, the ERISA Industry Committee (ERIC), and the Council for Communication Management. Al has more than 25 years of experience in the communication field and has been involved with many HR communication campaigns. Recently, he served as a senior communication resource for organizational change and global equity initiatives.

Timothy J. Sparks

Timothy J. Sparks is general counsel for Callisma, Inc., a network services consulting company based in Palo Alto, CA. Before joining Callisma, Mr. Sparks was a partner at Wilson Sonsini Goodrich & Rosati, P.C. in Palo Alto, CA, where he was the head of that firm's employee benefits and compensation group and a member of the firm's executive committee. Mr. Sparks frequently lectures throughout the country on equity and executive compensation topics and is a member of the National Association of Stock Plan Professionals (NASPP) Advisory Board. He received his undergraduate degree from U.C. Berkeley in 1980 and his law degree from U.C. Hastings College of the Law in 1983.

Ryan Weeden

Ryan Weeden is a project director at the National Center for Employee Ownership (NCEO). He leads the NCEO's international activities and codirects research and equity compensation activities. Mr. Weeden holds a M.A. in Public Policy from the University of Wisconsin-Madison and is a Certified Equity Professional (CEP) through Santa Clara University. He has coauthored several publications on the subject and is a frequent speaker at national and international meetings and conferences.

About the NCEO

The National Center for Employee Ownership (NCEO) is widely considered to be "the single best source of information on employee ownership anywhere in the world" (*Inc.* magazine, August 2000). Established in 1981 as a nonprofit information and membership organization, the NCEO now has over 3,000 members, including companies, professionals, unions, government officials, academics, and interested individuals. It is funded entirely through the work it does. The NCEO publishes a variety of materials explaining how employee ownership plans work, describing how to get employees more involved, and reviewing the research in this field. In addition, the NCEO holds approximately 50 workshops and conferences on employee ownership annually. The NCEO's work also includes extensive contacts with the media. Finally, in addition to publishing its own extensive line of books, the NCEO has written or edited five books for outside publishers during the 1980s and 1990s. The NCEO maintains an extensive Web site at *www.nceo.org*.

NCEO Membership Benefits

NCEO members receive the following benefits:

- The bimonthly newsletter, *Employee Ownership Report,* which covers ESOPs, stock options, and employee participation.
- Access to the members-only area of the NCEO Web site, including the NCEO's referral service, a searchable database of over 200 service providers.
- Substantial discounts on publications and events produced by the NCEO (such as this book).
- The right to telephone or e-mail the NCEO for answers to general or specific questions regarding employee ownership.

Membership Fees

For continuing members, yearly fees are as follows:

$70   *Associate* (non-employee ownership companies, organizations, and consultants not listed in the referral service)

$240   *Consultants* (listed in the referral service)

Employee Ownership Companies:
$70   1–50 employees
$125   51–100 employees
$240   101–500 employees
$350   Over 500 employees

Add $10 to any of the above amounts if your mailing address is outside North America.

Flat Rate for Introductory Membership

Regardless of the above subcategories (such as the $350 rate for large employee-owned companies), an introductory one-year NCEO membership is simply $70 ($80 if outside North America), or $30 for full-time students or faculty members ($40 if outside North America).

How to Join the NCEO

To join the NCEO, simply pay the introductory membership fee ($70, etc.) and provide your name, organizational name, and contact information. See the order form at the end of this section or go to our Web site at *www.nceo.org*.

NCEO Publications

The NCEO offers a variety of publications on all aspects of employee ownership and participation, from employee stock ownership plans (ESOPs) to stock options to employee participation. Following are descriptions of some of our main publications in these areas.

We publish new books and revise old ones on a yearly basis. To obtain the most current information on what we have available, visit our extensive Web site at *www.nceo.org* or call us at 510-208-1300.

Stock Options and Related Plans

- *The Stock Options Book* is a comprehensive resource covering the legal, tax, and design issues involved in implementing a broad-based stock option plan. It is our main book on the subject.
  Cost: $25 for NCEO members, $35 for nonmembers

- *Stock Options: Beyond the Basics* is more advanced and specialized than *The Stock Options Book*. It begins with a detailed overview of the field, followed by chapters on specialized topics such as repricing and evergreen options, and ends with a lengthy glossary.
  Cost: $25 for NCEO members, $35 for nonmembers

- *Model Equity Compensation Plans* provides examples of the plans discussed in the *Stock Options Book* (incentive stock option, nonqualified stock option, stock purchase, and phantom stock plans), together with brief explanations and a diskette with the plan documents.
  Cost: $50 for NCEO members, $75 for nonmembers

- This book, *Employee Stock Purchase Plans*, covers how ESPPs work; tax and legal issues; administration; accounting; communicating the plan to employees; and research on what companies are doing with their plans. The book includes sample plan documents.

  Cost: $25 for NCEO members, $35 for nonmembers

- *Current Practices in Stock Option Plan Design* is the full report on our survey of companies with broad-based stock option plans. It includes a detailed examination of plan design, use, and experience broken down by industry, size, and region. The book also discusses other research.

  Cost: $50 for NCEO members, $75 for nonmembers

- *Incentive Compensation and Employee Ownership* takes a broad look at how companies can use incentives, ranging from stock plans to cash bonuses to gainsharing, to motivate and reward employees. Includes both technical discussions and case studies.

  Cost: $25 for NCEO members, $35 for nonmembers

- *Equity-Based Compensation for Multinational Corporations* describes how companies can use stock options and other equity-based programs across the world to reward a global work force.

  Cost: $25 for NCEO members, $35 for nonmembers

- *Communicating Stock Options* offers practical ideas and information about how to explain stock options to a broad group of employees. It includes the views of experienced practitioners as well as detailed examples of how companies communicate tax consequences, financial information, and other matters to employees.

  Cost: $35 for NCEO members, $50 for nonmembers

- *Stock Options, Corporate Performance, and Organizational Change* presents the first serious research to examine the relationship between broadly granted stock options and company performance, and the extent of employee involvement in broad option companies.

  Cost: $15 for NCEO members, $25 for nonmembers

ESOPs

- *The ESOP Reader* is a general overview of the issues involved in establishing and operating an ESOP. It covers the basics of ESOP rules, feasibility, valuation, and other matters, and then discusses managing an ESOP company, including brief case studies. The book is intended for publicly traded companies and anyone with a general interest in ESOPs and employee participation.
  Cost: $25 for NCEO members, $35 for nonmembers

- *Selling to an ESOP* is a guide for owners, managers, and advisors of closely held businesses. It explains how ESOPs work and then offers a comprehensive look at legal structures, feasibility, valuation, financing (including self-financing), and other matters, especially the tax-deferred section 1042 "rollover" that allows owners to indefinitely defer capital gains taxation on the proceeds of the sale to the ESOP.
  Cost: $25 for NCEO members, $35 for nonmembers

- *Leveraged ESOPs and Employee Buyouts* discusses how ESOPs borrow money to buy out entire companies, purchase shares from a retiring owner, or finance new capital. Beginning with a primer on leveraged ESOPs and their uses, it then discusses contribution limits, valuation, multi-investor buyouts, legal due diligence, transaction structures, accounting, feasibility studies, financing sources, and more. It is applicable to both public and closely held companies.
  Cost: $25 for NCEO members, $35 for nonmembers

- The *Employee Ownership Q&A Disk* gives Microsoft Windows users (any version from Windows 3.1 onward) point-and-click access to 500 questions and answers on all aspects of ESOPs in a fully searchable hypertext format. (Note: this is for the general reader and is not a legal reference.) The keyword search allows users to search the entire file in seconds and see all the search "hits" in context. Distributed on a 1.44 MB 3.5-inch diskette.
  Cost: $75 for NCEO members, $100 for nonmembers

- The *ESOP Communications Sourcebook* is a looseleaf publication for ESOP companies. It includes ideas, reproducible forms, and examples on how to share financial information, explain ESOP features, and produce events to create an "ownership culture." It also addresses marketing employee ownership to customers.
  Cost: $35 for NCEO members, $50 for nonmembers

- The *ESOP Committee Guide* describes the different types of ESOP committees, the range of goals they can address, alternative structures, member selection criteria, training, committee life cycle concerns, and other issues.
  Cost: $20 for NCEO members, $30 for nonmembers

Other

- *Theory O: Creating an Ownership Style of Management* discusses how a company with an employee ownership plan can develop a better, more productive workplace through employee participation programs. Includes both a practical discussion of critical issues and 20 detailed case studies. Most of the companies that are discussed are ESOP companies, but a few use stock options.
  Cost: $20 for NCEO members, $30 for nonmembers

- *Section 401(k) Plans and Employee Ownership* focuses on how company stock is used in 401(k) plans, both in stand-alone 401(k) plans and combination 401(k)–ESOP plans ("KSOPs"). It addresses a whole range of issues that arise, including plan design, KSOPs, special techniques such as the "switchback," employee participation, and so on.
  Cost: $25 for NCEO members, $35 for nonmembers

- *The Journal of Employee Ownership Law and Finance* is the only professional journal solely devoted to employee ownership. Articles are written by leading experts and cover ESOPs, stock options, and related subjects in depth.

The *Journal* appears four times a year and typically is about 125 pages long.

Cost for one-year subscription:
$75 for NCEO members, $100 for nonmembers

To join the NCEO as a member or to order the above publications, mail or fax the order form on the last page of this book, use the secure ordering system on our Web site at *www.nceo.org*, or telephone us at (510) 208-1300 with your credit card in hand.

If you are not already a member but join at the same time you order publications, you will receive the members-only publication discounts.

Order Form

To order, fill out this form and mail it with your credit card information or check to the NCEO at 1736 Franklin Street, 8th Floor, Oakland, CA 94612; fax it with your credit card information to the NCEO at 510-272-9510; telephone us at 510-208-1300 with your credit card in hand; or order securely online at our Web site, *www.nceo.org*. If you are not already a member, you can join now to receive member discounts on the publications you order.

Name

Organization

Address

City, State, Zip (Country)

Telephone   Fax   E-mail

Method of Payment: ❏ Check (payable to "NCEO")   ❏ Visa   ❏ M/C   ❏ AMEX

Credit Card Number

Signature   Exp. Date

Checks are accepted only for orders from the U.S. and must be in U.S. currency.

Title	Qty.	Price	Total

Subtotal	$
Sales Tax	$
Shipping	$
Membership	$
TOTAL DUE	$

Tax: California residents add 8.25% sales tax (on publications only, not membership)

Shipping: First publication $4, each additional $1 ($15 each outside the U.S.)

Introductory NCEO Membership: $70 for one year ($80 outside North America)